# Pictures in Glass Frames

a Devotional

*Many Blessings,*
*Shawn B Jones*
*9/4/20*

**Shawn R. Jones**

## Ambassador International
GREENVILLE, SOUTH CAROLINA & BELFAST, NORTHERN IRELAND

www.ambassador-international.com

# Pictures in Glass Frames
## A Devotional

Printed in the United States of America

ISBN: 9781935507864

Scripture quoted is in NIV unless otherwise noted.

Cover Design by Matthew Mulder
Page Layout by Kelley Moore of Points & Picas

AMBASSADOR INTERNATIONAL
Emerald House
427 Wade Hampton Blvd.
Greenville, SC 29609, USA
www.ambassador-international.com

AMBASSADOR BOOKS
The Mount
2 Woodstock Link
Belfast, BT6 8DD, Northern Ireland, UK
www.ambassador-international.com

*The colophon is a trademark of Ambassador*

# Dedication

For my husband, Jeffrey H. Jones,
the most devoted person I know

"This unique devotional. . . is superbly written with a warmth and sincerity that requires introspection and encourages a deeper relationship with God."

—Cecilia B Dennery, Christian educator and author

"Shawn Regina Jones' devotional collection, *Pictures in Glass Frames,* is filled with healing and insight. Jones' narratives rend richer and deeper for their compassionate and honest telling. This devotional is excellent for personal growth, or group study."

—Leah Maines, award winning, and
regional bestselling author

# Contents

# Acknowledgments

Special thanks . . .

- To God for being everything I will ever need.

- To my husband and best friend, Jeffrey, for being loving, selfless, and supportive of all my endeavors.

- To my children, Jeffrey and Jade, for reading my manuscript, offering editorial suggestions, allowing me to share their lives, and encouraging me consistently.

- To my mother, Rhonda Fitzgerald, for allowing me to share her life with others, believing in me, and raising me with confidence and humility.

- To my sister, Rashonda Robinson, for prayer, daily encouragement, and legal advice.

- To my Bishop, Dr. S. Todd Townsend, for life-changing sermons, prayer, encouragement, and a heartfelt endorsement.

- To Elder Cecilia Dennery for doing an outstanding job editing my manuscript before I sent it to publishers and also for writing a wonderful endorsement.

- To Leah Maines for her kind spirit, ongoing encouragement, and beautiful endorsement.

- To Rev. Dr. James Woods, First Lady Barbara Woods, Beverly Cardwell, and Women with a Vision of El Shaddai Christian Assembly for inviting me to give my testimony and share my devotional before it was accepted for publication.

- To Teresa Walston for laying hands on me and leaving a beautiful impression on my life.

- To Pamela Cruz, an awesome prayer warrior, for praying for me and encouraging me Mother's Day weekend.

- To Jeffrey H. Jones for taking a great author's photo.

- To Lorraine Castle for giving me the assignment to write a devotion a day.

- To Melanie Kelly for giving me my first large audience.

- To Crystal Waters-Reaves for her infectious strength and encouragement during the times I needed it the most.

- To my sister, Rhonda I. Fitzgerald and friends, Tanya Cain and Frieda Bervine, for their support and encouragement.

- To Karenanne Brown, Frank Champine, Renee' Fernandez, Rafael Green, Sharae Mack, Kiana Jones-Peoples, and Cynthia Sabol for reading the manuscript and giving readers' comments.

- To anyone who has ever encouraged me along the way with a prayer, kind word, or smile.

- To the outstanding Ambassador International staff for their professionalism and expertise.

# When the Glass Breaks

His plan will
come to fruition
regardless
of your
circumstances.

# 1

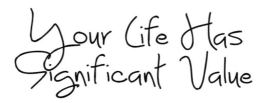

Surely I was sinful at birth, sinful from the time my mother conceived me.

Psalm 51:5

I wasn't born into the best circumstances. My mother was seventeen years old, on her way to college on a full scholarship. When she became pregnant, my grandmother was devastated. Too poor to pay the doctor to perform an illegal abortion, they experimented with pills, Tanqueray Gin, turpentine, and boiling water. When the popular home remedy failed, my mother was sent to live with her uncle and aunt in Hartford, Connecticut. She was supposed to put me up for adoption, return home to Atlantic City, and prepare to leave for Howard University in the fall. However, when she was eight months pregnant, she changed her mind and refused to sign the adoption papers.

My great uncle and aunt sympathized with their niece, but they still felt she was too young to handle the responsibilities of motherhood. They offered to adopt me, hoping my mother would feel more comfortable knowing her baby would be reared by someone in the family. To their surprise, my mother refused their offer, and much to my grandmother's dismay, her college-bound daughter returned home with a baby.

My grandmother had reason to be concerned. My mother was poor, unmarried, and knew very little about parenting, but when I came into her life, she gave me the best that she had. My mother also wanted the best for herself. When I was in Head Start, she went back to school. Four years later, she graduated from Rutgers–Camden with honors and used her education to educate me. She also sent me to dancing school, read the Bible to me daily, and kissed me every night before bed. Not once in my childhood did I feel unwanted or unloved, so when she told me about the circumstances surrounding her pregnancy and my birth, I was shocked but not angry.

You may wonder why I know this story and why I'm sharing it with you. First, I know this story because my mother understood that sharing her darkest moments with me would strengthen our bond, and I, in turn, would not be afraid to come to her with my own transgressions. Second, it is important for you to know that over four decades ago, God decided that I should live. He had a plan for me even though I was "unplanned," and He definitely has a plan for you. God can work anything out for you, and His plan will come to fruition regardless of your circumstances.

*Dear Lord, please teach me to cherish my life. Remind me that You have a wonderful plan for me even though I was born in sin, and thank You for Your divine virtue that is more powerful than my worst transgressions. Amen.*

# 2

# Restore My Mind

For God hath not given us the spirit of fear; but of power,
and of love, and of a sound mind.

2 Timothy 1:7 (KJV)

Have you ever been afraid of what the day might bring? I have,
and to be honest it was more of a moment to moment struggle.
My mind would not stop creating visions of unforeseen tragedies,
and my fears increasingly turned into panic. It got so bad that I
would get lightheaded as soon as I walked into what I believed was
a potentially dangerous situation. The major problem was that everything had become a potentially dangerous situation to me. My
house was the only place I felt safe. Then one day, while driving, I
lost control of my body. I gripped the steering wheel several times,
trying to find a position to calm me. I grabbed my neck and hair
repeatedly, alternating between the two with my mouth twitch-
ing, my hands and arms shaking. I looked over at a group of boys
selling drugs on the corner, and at that moment, I understood the
tremendous struggle within every drug addict, alcoholic, and crazy
person I had ever seen in my life. I even thought of pulling my car
over to the curb where the boys stood and buying something—
anything—to make me feel better.

That day, I realized I couldn't get well on my own. I couldn't beat the invisible power that had a hold on me. My mind had folded in on itself. In six months, I had become both depressed and paranoid, and I knew I could no longer think my way back to reality. All the cliché prayers I had learned went right out the window. Instead, I cried a deep cry, gargling Jesus' name through my tears.

In the days that followed, God gave me deep human insight and overwhelming compassion for people I had once casually dismissed, like prostitutes and the neighborhood "crack head." Whenever I encountered them, I talked to each of them about God. I discovered they had a story that was not too different from my own. Life, with its magnitude of cruelty, had brought each of them down to the place where I met them on the street. Instantly I understood that God put them in my path so I could look beyond their plight and connect with their humanity. Thus, I was able to pray for them as fervently as I prayed for myself and humbly submit my mind to the Lord.

In the months that followed, I read the Bible consistently, and God made His presence known every moment I had doubt. Today, I am still sustained by His Word and my personal relationship with Him, as He gives me the courage to face each new day. Jesus can do the same for you. So, even if the day brings an unexpected trial, know assuredly that you can trust the Lord.

*Dear Lord, reassure me that I do not have to be afraid of anything. Remind me that You are the master of my thoughts and restorer of my mind. Courageously, I walk in Your perfect will. Thank You for being my God. Amen.*

3

# You're Never "Good Enough" for God

For by the grace given me I say to every one of you: Do
not think of yourself more highly than you ought, but
rather think of yourself with sober judgment. . . .

Romans 12:3

There was a time when I didn't think I needed to go to church
because I believed I was morally "good enough." I felt church
was for morally corrupt people like habitual liars, thieves, and
adulterers. Since I didn't fit into any of those categories, I didn't
think I needed to have a closer relationship with God. Then, I
was faced with a problem I couldn't handle or solve. I had become
severely depressed, and for the first time I felt I had no control
over my life.

I confided in a friend, and she invited me to her church. The
evening before I went, I thought, *Why do I need someone reading
scripture to me when I can read it for myself? I have a brain just like they
have a brain.* Then, I opened the Bible and read Romans 12:1–3.
I thought it was a coincidence and found it almost laughable that
it seemed to be speaking directly to me. When I went to church

the next day, the pastor preached on the same verses I had read the night before. He broke the scripture down word by word and repeated my thoughts like a mind reader. I realized, then, that it was not a coincidence—and it was no laughing matter.

Week after week, my "small" sins were magnified. I could no longer pretend they were not negatively affecting my life. Sunday after Sunday, it became so clear. I felt like my most private thoughts were spewed from the pulpit, but I kept going to church because I needed God to deliver me from my depression. I repeatedly asked God to heal me, but instead He kept fixing my character. It's not that He wasn't revealing Himself to me in various other ways. He was. As a matter of fact, He was blessing me in many areas of my life, but I didn't fully appreciate it because He wouldn't answer my one specific prayer. All I wanted to do was go back to feeling normal again.

Thankfully, I never went back to "normal" because I discovered that "normal" is below God's standards. God refused to give me back the mind I prayed for incessantly. Instead, He gave me a brand new, humble mind that knows it can never be "good enough" for Him.

If you don't think you need to go to church, maybe a part of you also feels you're "good enough." However, if you decide to go to church weekly and spend quality time with God every day, you will experience a fulfillment that exceeds the satisfaction you get from moral goodness. Although a "good enough" life can be pleasurable, it cannot compare to a life overflowing with God's presence.

*Dear Lord, please remove prideful thoughts from my mind and remind me that "good enough" is never enough. Please keep me both humbled and encouraged as I fully submit myself to You. Amen.*

# 4

# Love God First

Anyone who loves their father or mother more than me is not worthy of me; anyone who loves their son or daughter more than me is not worthy of me. Whoever does not take up their cross and follow me is not worthy of me.

Matthew 10:37–38

My daughter was born two months premature. Several babies in the neonatal care unit had developed a contagious respiratory infection, and two of them died. I watched the mothers mourn as I held my own child tightly in my arms. I prayed incessantly, and my daughter did not catch the infection. However, there was one medical problem after another that lengthened her hospital stay. She was fed through a tube in her nose. She had an IV in her forehead, and tubes and wires extended from her tiny body like extra pairs of limbs. It was too much for me to bear with my limited experience as a mother and a Christian. Family members attempted to emotionally prepare me for my daughter's death, but nothing they said mattered to me. I needed to change my feelings toward God because I realized that I loved my husband and children more than I loved Jesus.

I assumed my husband felt the same way and would justify my feelings, so I told him, "I love you more than I love Jesus, and I love our children more than I love Jesus." I saw a mixture of fear and disappointment on my husband's face, but I continued, "Do you know why? Because I know you. I don't *know* Jesus, but I do know if *you* had the power to heal our daughter, you would. God has that power," I cried hopelessly, "so why is He putting us through this?"

He responded simply yet profoundly, "God doesn't make mistakes, and He loves her more than we could ever imagine. She's His child first, and if He takes her, she was His to begin with."

That was the last thing I wanted to hear my husband say, but back then, what did I know about God's infinite grace? Today, I can't imagine loving anyone more than I love Jesus. If that sounds strange to you, I understand. At first it was very strange for me too, but over the years, life has been too unpredictable and people have come and gone too often for me to love anyone more than I love Christ. If you have not done so already, I pray that today you too will come to the same realization.

God is worthy. Love Him first.

*Dear Lord, please teach me how to love You first. If there is anyone that I love more than I love You, please bring it to my attention. I want to make sure You are the first love of my life. Amen.*

# 5

# Money Is Not Enough

People, despite their wealth, do not endure; they are like the beasts that perish. That is the fate of those who trust in themselves, and of their followers, who approve their sayings.

Psalm 49:12–13

As I watched my four-year-old daughter in the small bed in the recovery room at Children's Hospital, I thought, *Even if I had 500 million dollars, I couldn't change this situation.* I was her mother. It was my job to make sure she was happy and healthy and to make sure life was as beautiful as it could possibly be for her. I had bought her everything I possibly could to give her some highs to balance out the lows of her circumstances. I had even promised God I would move back to the housing projects and sell all my belongings if He would just heal her. I began to resent everything I owned because I never asked God for material wealth. I asked Him for a healing, and I was willing to barter or pay for it with the very same possessions I had come to resent. However, I knew that God wanted me to rely solely on my faith.

Standing in the hospital that day, I knew I needed God to help me cope from one second to the next. My insides were trembling so much I could barely stand, and I knew I was going to collapse if I did not get a grip on my emotions. I needed Jesus to get me through, and when I called on Him, each cell inside of me responded to His name. My body relaxed, and He covered me with His incomparable peace.

After several visits to Children's Hospital, I looked at life much differently. Money became less important to me. More than anything else, I wanted to have a closer relationship with the God Who helped me stand during the most helpless moments of my life. Money could not be my god—after watching my daughter sleep with machines beeping by her side and wires extending from her gown, I knew it could never be god for me. Although it was something I had always known on the surface, I had finally internalized it with this weighty experience.

What experience has taught you that money is not enough? Long after the experience had passed, did you forget how worthless money was to you during that time? There will be times in your life when you need much more than money to get you through. Money is useful, but it cannot sustain you in every crisis—an ongoing relationship with Christ is invaluable in all circumstances.

*Dear Lord, teach me to trust You more than I trust people and money, and continually remind me that material wealth can never replace You because You are the wealth of the world Who generously offers His priceless grace. Amen.*

6

# Call His Name

Therefore God exalted him to the highest place and gave him the name that is above every name, that at the name of Jesus every knee should bow, in heaven and on earth and under the earth.

Philippians 2:9–10

In the middle of the night, I awoke with severe stomach cramps. It became so unbearable I thought I might pass out from the pain. I prayed a broken prayer in between groans, twisting back and forth beneath the sheet. I didn't want to wake my husband and tell him how I felt because then I would be accepting the fact that I was *really* sick. Unfortunately, I seemed to get sicker by the minute. Then the lyrics to a popular gospel song came to my mind. I could hear the mass choir singing Jesus' name over and over again. I stopped twisting and moaning, placed my hands over my abdomen, and whispered "Jesus" repeatedly until the power of His name eased my pain and lulled me to sleep.

If you are ever in unbearable physical or emotional pain, repeat Jesus' name softly. Concentrate on its sound and remind yourself that He is more powerful than your situation. You may feel overwhelmed and afraid, but Jesus is not intimidated by the severity of your circumstances. Call on Him whenever you are hurting, because Jesus' name exudes healing, power, and peace.

*Dear Lord, when I am tempted to use Your name inappropriately, please remind me of its sacred power and divine significance. Teach me to always revere and secure its power. Amen.*

# 1

# Your Heart Aches

"Very truly I tell you," Jesus answered, "before Abraham was born, I am!"

John 8:58

We often experience significant heartache when our romantic relationships end. Nothing positive seems to stir inside us, and we have to manage debilitating emotions as we try to function normally throughout the day; even ordinary tasks become difficult. However, if we look around, there are other people living happily without that person. If our next-door neighbor can live without him and someone on the other side of the globe can live without her, we can too. The person we long for does not possess all-pervading love, mercy, and understanding, yet we sometimes want them back desperately in spite of their human insufficiencies. In those times, we must look beyond the loss of our earthly relationship and focus on the permanency of our relationship with Jesus. God promised He would never leave us or forsake us (Hebrews 13:5), and He has kept His word.

Jesus has always been there for us. He was there long before Abraham, Moses, and Adam. He was there with divine authority and capability before God created humanity. So, why do we obsess over the absence of someone who is not God? We sometimes do this because God is not always the center of our lives before we fall in love, and when our romantic relationship ends, we fail to realize that our relationship with God is the most secure relationship we will ever have.

I must confess I have done this a few times myself. Before I was married, I fell in and out of love. After the relationships ended, I didn't know how I was going to go on. My first relationship was the most difficult. After we dated exclusively for a year, my boyfriend told me he was in love with a man. I was sixteen years old, and I had no idea how to mentally process his confession. I was devastated. I remember sitting in front of the mirror, watching myself cry and sing "Until You Come Back to Me" by Luther Vandross. I crooned pathetically through my tears, trying desperately to harmonize the pain away. It took me six months and constant prayer to get over him, so I am a witness that the hurt is real.

If you are devastated over a breakup, I am not trying to trivialize your pain. I just want you to know that Jesus will love you safely and securely. He will never leave you. God is love (1 John 4:8), and He loves you. He will always love you. That is why you have to make God your first love, and rest assured that He will choose your second.

> *Dear Lord, help me devote my life to You, and forgive me for the times I have ignored You and worshipped people. I am sorry for all the times I have taken You for granted. You are the only One Who has always been there, and I am eternally grateful for Your presence. Please fill the voids in my life with Your consistent and perfect love. Amen.*

# 8

# Pray for Your Enemies

Do not gloat when your enemy falls; when they stumble, do not let your heart rejoice.

Proverbs 24:17

My Aunt Gwen was in her mid-forties when her husband, Bruce, ran off with Monica, her close friend. To make matters more painful and complicated, Bruce and Monica had a baby together. Aunt Gwen prayed herself through the ordeal. She even prayed for her husband, his mistress, and their newborn son. Although my aunt was emotionally distraught, she believed God would be there for her, but she had to constantly remind herself that vengeance is the Lord's (Romans 12:19). After a while, Aunt Gwen's body started to respond to the pressure. Black leather bags formed under her eyes from crying and lack of sleep, and sometimes she would be so distressed her room would spin wildly as she leaned on her bed with one hand, trying to steady herself.

However, she prayed continually, and God sustained her and improved her life in her husband's absence. She and her four children were continually blessed. She moved into a new home surrounded by an acre of land and stately trees, and her children were happy and enjoyed the amenities of their new neighborhood. In the meantime, Bruce and Monica broke up. Sickness and depression plagued Monica's family. Similarly, Bruce's life lacked peace and he too became ill.

A decade later, Monica came to Aunt Gwen and apologized. She told my aunt that she had recently been establishing a close relationship with Christ. She asked for Aunt Gwen's forgiveness, and my aunt forgave and embraced both Monica and her son. She even took Monica's son out to lunch and often invited him to her home. I was amazed by Aunt Gwen's compassion. Not once did she celebrate when Monica described how difficult life had gotten for her and how unbearable her circumstances had become. I sometimes wonder where Aunt Gwen would be today if she had held on to the pain, if she had allowed herself to become bitter and unforgiving. It is an amazing story of forgiveness and a true example of how Christ would like us to react toward people who have hurt us.

Is there someone you have not considered praying for because they hurt you? Do you know Jesus loves them just as much as He loves you? He expects you to love them too. God understands that it is not an easy task, but we are His children, and He has freely shared His divine compassion with us. Therefore, we have the God-given ability to love and pray for all our enemies.

*Dear Lord, help me realize that my enemies are probably in much more pain than they could have ever caused me or anyone else. Remind me that life may be more difficult for them than I could ever imagine, and please teach me to have mercy on them as often as You have had mercy on me. Amen.*

# Do Not Tolerate Abuse

Follow God's example . . . and walk in the way of love. . . .

Ephesians 5:1–2

One Christian woman explained to me that she tolerates her abusive husband because she is trying to be a submissive wife. Even though her husband is physically abusive and has had several extramarital affairs, she refuses to leave him. I know the Lord does not want her or anyone else to submit to such cruelty. When she confided in me, I reminded her that the Bible instructs husbands to "love their wives as their own bodies" (Ephesians 5:28). When you read Ephesians 5:22–32, note that it does not say your spouse is supposed to mistreat you, so if you are a man or woman who is being physically, emotionally, or psychologically abused, you need to get help. It is not fair to you, and if you have children, it is certainly not fair to them.

I feel very strongly about this because the most ugly and unforgettable memories of my childhood are watching my father abuse my mother. I remember how his fury shook the walls of our cramped apartment and rattled in my small chest whenever he came home. At first, my mother was too afraid to fight back, but then she realized he would probably kill her if she did not defend herself.

The very last time my father came after my mother, she stood on the bed, holding a heavy lamp over his head. After that episode, he didn't come home too often, and eventually he left for good. Do you know why he finally left? He could no longer control her. She refused to be a victim.

I am not suggesting that you should abuse the perpetrator. You can fight back in ways that are safe and legal. During the time of my parents' relationship, there were not as many places for victims of domestic violence to go. Actually, I am not sure if there were any, but today, there are multiple agencies that help both male and female victims of domestic abuse. Research the agencies in your area, and ask God to help you take that first step to a better life.

> *Dear Lord, please give me the strength I need to change my present situation because I know it is not Your will for me to be abused or mistreated in any way. Guide me through the journey of seeking a better life for myself, and please keep me safe. Amen.*

# 10

# Difficult Trials and God's Will

Then Jesus went with his disciples to a place called Gethsemane, and he said to them . . . "My soul is overwhelmed with sorrow to the point of death. Stay here and keep watch with me." Going a little farther, he fell with his face to the ground and prayed, "My Father, if it is possible, may this cup be taken from me. Yet not as I will, but as you will."

Matthew 26:36–39

Is the intensity of Jesus' prayer familiar to you? If it is, and you have to go through a difficult situation, pray that God's will be done. Sometimes God's will involves us going through a difficult process. For example, I had to have surgery a few years ago. I fasted and prayed for the Lord to miraculously remove the tumors from my body. He confirmed that I *had* to go through with the procedure. I went through with it, and there were complications the evening of my surgery. I developed a fever, which alarmed my husband and the hospital staff. As my husband rubbed my hair, I assured him, "Honey, I'm fine. . . ."

The nurse interrupted, glaring at the thermometer, "No, this is not good." She turned and walked out of the room.

"Don't pay her any mind," I said. "She doesn't know what she's talking about." My husband didn't look convinced. I continued, "God told me to have this procedure done. I got three confirmations." Then I thought, *I'm on a morphine drip; nobody's going to take me seriously.*

Even after I was released from the hospital, I continued to have complications. My blood pressure went up. My fever was up and down for a week. I broke out in hives and woke up in the middle of the night unable to breathe. It was awful, but, looking back, I value the experience because it showed me the true vulnerability of my flesh. It reminded me how much I need the Lord's protection and healing. It was a humbling event that made me more open to receive God's glory.

*Dear Lord, I know the trials I must endure are for the betterment of my relationship with You. I know You will never leave me to scramble in the hardships I must face on earth. I can persist because Christ lives in me, so strengthen and prepare me for the journey and humble me for the victory. Amen.*

# Reframing Your Picture

PURPOSELY KEEP
YOUR MIND
ON JESUS.

# Are You Sleeping?

But about that day or hour no one knows, not even the angels in heaven, nor the Son, but only the Father. If he comes suddenly, do not let him find you sleeping.

Mark 13:32, 36

In our busy human lives we fail to ponder the responsibilities of God's creations. We see flowers and birds and trees almost every day, but we seldom focus on their detailed significance. For example, flowers make nectar. Nectar is food for various pollinators, including insects, birds, and bats. Similarly, water evaporates from bodies of water. Water comes back to earth as rain. Rain waters trees. Trees give off oxygen. *Everything* has a purpose. Even *animal* waste fertilizes the earth. Everything inside and outside us is part of a cycle of divine creation.

So, what is it that you have been put on earth to do? Surely, God has given you an assignment too, and when you fail to produce, something is left undone. Something is left uncreated, uninvestigated, unexplored, or unprotected because of you. You are an essential part of creation too, and there is something left unfinished that only you can do.

*Dear Lord, if You return in my lifetime, I don't want You to catch me sleeping. I want my days to be filled with purpose so my years will be useful to Your heavenly kingdom and Your earthly creation. You can trust me with the jobs You have assigned me to do. I am ready to complete them for Your glory. Amen.*

12

# God Will Get You There

Ants are creatures of little strength, yet they store up their food in the summer.

Proverbs 30:25

One summer morning, my son and I were walking through a park in the city. He spotted an anthill and kicked it with his small sandaled foot.

I asked him, "Jeffrey, why did you do that? Do you know what that is?"

He knew what it was, but, understandably, his toddler mentality could not explain why he had kicked the anthill. I reprimanded him. His little face was remorseful after I told him how hard ants worked and how sad he would feel if a giant stepped on our home.

Then, I took the lesson a step further. We followed an ant carrying a crumb across the park for over an hour. Even I could not believe the diligence and perseverance God had given the small creature! The lesson was for both my son and me, and we were fascinated during the entire length of the ant's journey. The ant dropped the crumb a few times and picked it back up. Boys rode by on bikes, and my son was afraid the ant was going to get run over. The ant ran into one obstacle after another, facing many new dangers, but finally he made it to his destination, an ant hole quite a distance away from where he began.

I don't know what your destination is today or what purpose God has for you, but do not get discouraged on your journey. Even if you have not found the energy to start, prepare. Then, take small steps forward, and God *will* get you there.

> *Dear Lord, thank You for showing me that I don't have to be the smartest, strongest, or fastest person around to get things done efficiently. You created me, and because of that I have everything I need to live a joyous and purposeful life. You possess divine strength and intellect, so all I have to do is follow You. Thank You for loving me for who I am and giving me the perseverance and consistency I need to reach my destination. Amen.*

# 13

# Daily Tasks

And we know that in all things God works for the good of those who love him, who have been called according to his purpose.

Romans 8:28

There are many tasks you don't want to finish because they are tedious, mundane, or difficult, so you complete them thoughtlessly and, sometimes, unhappily. With this frame of mind, eventually each day folds ungracefully into the next without real meaning for you. As a result, you grumble about each item on your schedule without realizing that grumbling actually makes you more frustrated.

From now on, whenever you feel a need to complain, focus on your blessings. Look forward to each day with a new attitude by honoring God in your daily tasks even when your responsibilities are mundane, tedious, mentally draining, or downright backbreaking. However, to honor God consistently, you have to purposely keep your mind on Jesus. You can start by keeping your home and car stereo systems on Christian radio stations, reading the Bible at the beginning and end of your day, and keeping a devotional with you at work. Putting those few suggestions into action will strengthen your relationship with God and give Him an opening to communicate with you in various ways throughout the day.

For now, examine the purpose of your daily responsibilities. What will happen if you do not go to the market, wash clothes, or pay bills? What are the consequences of not going to the doctor, work, or school? Think about what would happen if you did not complete each of your daily tasks. I am sure you will discover that each task is a significant piece of a greater purpose.

*Dear Jesus, thank You for teaching me to look at my responsibilities differently, and thank You for caring about the small and large details of my life. Please teach me to be more grateful, caring, and mindful of You throughout the day. Amen.*

# 14

# Humble Me

To the weak I became weak, to win the weak. I have
become all things to all people so that by all possible
means I might save some.

1 Corinthians 9:22

When I was in my early twenties, I volunteered on South
Five, the psychiatric unit of Cooper Hospital. Mostly, I
organized games with the inpatients. One day while I was running a group, an elderly man referred to himself as "crazy." His
comment made me feel uneasy, so I interrupted the game and
talked candidly with the group.

"If you overwork any part of your body," I explained, "it
becomes sore, and your mind is no different. When you sprain
your ankle, you rest it, and sometimes you need medicine to help
ease the pain. It's the same thing with your mind. Sometimes
you just have to let it rest, and sometimes you need medicine to
help it rest."

I told them I had been depressed before, and they wanted to
know how I got better. I hesitated; I wasn't sure if I was allowed
to talk to them about God. After all, I was just a volunteer on
the ward. I decided to follow my instincts, and I told them I had

allowed Jesus to heal me. Before I knew it, I was sharing my life story and my deliverance.

After that day, I really looked forward to volunteering. Initially, I had volunteered because I was a psychology major at Rutgers and I thought I would have a greater chance of getting hired at the hospital after I got my degree. However, God had a different plan. While I was there, I learned how fragile the mind really is, and I also learned that the average person is only one tragic situation away from trading in their street clothes for hospital pajamas on South Five. The patients on the psych unit were ordinary folks who wanted the best for themselves and their families, and I was so humbled by interacting with them that I became a more sensitive and understanding person on and off the unit.

God used my years of volunteering to make me more compassionate and understanding toward those who are less fortunate. My experiences on South Five helped prepare me for ministry, just as God will use your experiences to prepare you for ministry. He will allow you to meet people in the midst of their troubles and use your God-given empathy to open their hearts to learn more about Jesus.

*Dear Lord, please teach me to be more like Jesus. Give me the empathy I need to relate to all people regardless of their situations so I can humbly lead them to You. Amen.*

# 15

# Follow Christ Like Children

"Truly I tell you, unless you change and become like little children, you will never enter the kingdom of heaven. Therefore, whoever takes the lowly position of this child is the greatest in the kingdom of heaven."

Matthew 18:3–4

Most children welcome adult leadership. They feel good knowing there is someone who will feed, clothe, love, and instruct them. However, when some children become adults, they lose these childlike qualities and feel no one can tell them what to do because they think they have become their own leaders and can make their own decisions. They are also free to be creative or destructive. Even if they suffer the consequences of poor decisions, they are able to choose without parental intervention. Because of this freedom, some adults tend to believe they are masters of their own destinies, and, unfortunately, we live in a world that often promotes this belief.

Remember, the Bible warns us not to "conform to the pattern of this world, but be transformed by the renewing of your mind. Then you will be able to test and approve what God's will is—his good, pleasing and perfect will" (Romans 12:2). Since

God's will is perfect, He should be the only master of your destiny. Furthermore, He lives inside you, and His spirit guides you (Romans 8:9–11), but He requires you to be like a child and welcome His leadership into your life. Even though He has given you freewill, He wants you to use that freewill to submit to *His* will. The options are there, but the choice is yours. I pray you regain the humility to follow Christ like a child.

> *Dear Lord, I appreciate the freedom You have given me, but like a child needs his or her parent, I need You. Please reframe my thinking and teach me to rely solely on You. You are my Father, and I am Your child. I welcome Your guidance today, tomorrow, and forever. Amen.*

16

# A Good Name

A good name is more desirable than great riches; to be esteemed is better than silver or gold. Rich and poor have this in common: The Lord is the Maker of them all.

Proverbs 22:1–2

When people think of you, what comes to their minds? Self-examination is important; however, it is sometimes difficult to be an unbiased observer of oneself. Many people will form opinions of you based on your actions *and* on their thoughts and own personal feelings about themselves. Nevertheless, most people want to be seen as kind and honest. However, there are others who want to be known for their wealth and possessions. What kind of person are you? To which category do you belong? It's easy to get caught up in materialism because it seems like so little around us is spiritual anymore. And even the "spiritual" is looking more material lately. It's easy to lose focus.

The best way you can examine yourself is by using Christ as your example. Try to be Christlike in all you think, say, and do. Of course we have some excellent human role models to follow, but sometimes they fall short of what God wants them to be simply because they're human. After all, wealth sometimes woos people with the best intentions off their paths, and unfortunately many of us are easily influenced by people who have money. But I assure you, wealth is temporary. Money will not matter when you come face to face with Jesus, the true paragon of goodness. Live for God, and when He thinks of you, your name *will* be good.

> *Dear Lord, I want to have a good name. Please help me in my daily attempt to be the best Christian I can be. Thank you so much for Jesus, the perfect role model and everlasting example of kindness, peace, integrity, and love. Amen.*

# 17

# Predictable Dependability

When a man makes a vow to the Lord or takes an oath to obligate himself by a pledge, he must not break his word but must do everything he said.

Numbers 30:2

One rainy morning, I was waiting outside for an appointment. I knew I was going to be standing outside in the cold for at least ten minutes. The owner was always ten or more minutes late. However, I continued to come to every appointment on time. That particular morning, the owner called me on my cell phone and told me she was running an hour behind schedule. Now, what was I supposed to do? Go home and come back? Stand outside in the cold? Or just hang around town for an hour? I was so frustrated that I went to another establishment that provided the same service. Later that evening, I called the owner on the phone and told her I would not be returning to her company. She asked me to give her another chance, and she promised she would never be late again. As I predicted, she was on time for a while, and then she fell back into the same routine.

What is your routine? Are you consistently undependable and unreliable? Do you constantly make promises you don't keep? Are you involved in every activity you can imagine, giving a quarter of effort to every area of your life? Do people often have to pick up your slack because you are predictably unreliable? If that's how you operate, you are probably frustrating a lot of people. You need to make it a point to do what you say when you say you are going to do it.

Your word is important, and people need you to follow through. You are important to the people you are connected to. What you do and do not do always matters. It is better to say no than it is to make promises you can't keep. Promises are very important to God, especially the ones we make to Him. Today, practice keeping your word. Let your predictability be your dependability.

*Dear Lord, I want You to be able to count on me. I want You to be able to say,*

*"My servant, [your name], will do what I ask them to do." Lord, while I am working to better my relationship with You, please teach me to be a reliable and dependable member of society. Amen.*

# 18

# Nothing Is Private

There is nothing concealed that will not be disclosed, or hidden that will not be made known. What you have said in the dark will be heard in the daylight, and what you have whispered in the ear in the inner rooms will be proclaimed from the roofs.

Luke 12:2–3

When we are among family at home, we sometimes act and speak differently than we do in public because we know our loved ones are more tolerant of our shortcomings. For example, you may get angry at your sister and say something hurtful, but if you have a good relationship with her, you know you will work it out and still love each other at the end of the day. Because of the security we have in our familial bonds, we are more open with what we say and do in front of family. On the other hand, because of the insecurity we feel in public, we struggle to hide our imperfections from those who don't really know us.

Truly, God is the only One Who knows everything about us, yet we sometimes become preoccupied with other people's thoughts. Most people are not even thinking about us half the time because they are too busy trying not to put their own insecurities on public display. Of course we don't want to have a bad reputation, but we also don't want to obsessively worry about what others think of us. We have to find a balance between caring too much and not caring at all.

God is our balance. So instead of worrying about the thoughts of other people, who are often too self-absorbed to think about us too profoundly, we really need to care what *God* thinks. He is the only One Who knows us better than our family and closest friends do. He knows exactly what we are thinking, and He hears and sees everything we say and do.

With God, *nothing* is private.

*Dear Lord, deliver me from obsessing over what others think of me. Remind me that You are the only One Who can see me in my public and private life. Teach me to always be the me that is pleasing to You. Amen.*

# 19

# Follow God's Instruction

Now therefore hearken unto me, O ye children: for blessed are they that keep my ways. Hear instruction, and be wise, and refuse it not.

Proverbs 8:32–33 (KJV)

While I was working on my poetry chapbook, *Womb Rain,* I thought it was going to be the bestselling chapbook of all time. I was very optimistic even though it was my first book and I was an unknown author. I sold a few hundred copies in a few weeks, and then I sold only a few here and there. Then I started working on my book of devotions, and I thought it too was going to be a bestseller. To me, being blessed through my writing endeavor meant selling thousands of copies and becoming a well-known author. After all, I thought my book would be an instant success because I listened to God's instructions, even though I really didn't want to at first.

When I got the assignment, I thought, *Write a book of devotions when I could write a juicy novel and take a cheap shot at worldly fame? At least I know there's a huge market for sex and violence.* Well, thank God I had sense enough to know the enemy was trying to veer me off God's path. Still, once I started writing one devotion after another, I thought God would reward me handsomely in the end because I was obedient to Him. Then, one day I got a revelation. I believe it was God Who put the thought into my head because I was too focused on myself to think of it on my own. I thought, *If I only sell five books, I have done God's will. Those five books will improve five people's lives, and those five people will improve more people's lives.*

I finally understood that the Lord could not use me until I realized this project was not for my own recognition. It is for God's recognition, and I have shared intimate moments of my life with you because God wanted me to. So, if you happen to be one of 5, 500, or 5,000 readers, this is the Lord's gift to you, and I am honored that He has used me to deliver it. No amount of money could replace that honor, and I feel more blessed today than I have ever felt in my entire life because I have chosen God's will over my own.

> *Dear Lord, remind me that a blessed life is not necessarily a life of prominence and affluence. Continue to humble me so I can hear Your voice and follow Your divine instructions. Thank You, for I have found true success and blessedness in my relationship with You. Amen.*

# 20

# I Will Too

And his disciples came to him, and awoke him, saying, Lord, save us: we perish. And he saith unto them, Why are ye fearful, O ye of little faith? Then he arose, and rebuked the winds and the sea; and there was a great calm.

Matthew 8:25–26 (KJV)

My carnal desires do not matter. My selfish hopes, dreams, and fleshly motivations cannot compete with Your will. If the wind and sea obey You without ears to hear Your voice, eyes to read Your Word, or a mouth to praise Your name, who am I? Who do I think I am to ignore the daily call to serve You with all five senses You have given me? Who am I to disregard You with all the gifts and talents I borrow from You each day? If all of nature's elements respond to You, I will too.

*Dear Lord, You created me as You created both the wind and the sea, and You have blessed me with multiple senses to respond to Your voice. I am ready to listen to You and respond with the gifts You have given me to heed your call. Amen.*

# Cropping Your Photo

welcome
Divine elimination.

# 21

# Christian Confidence

"But what about you?" he asked. "Who do you say I am?"
Simon Peter answered, "You are the Messiah, the Son of
the living God." Jesus replied, "Blessed are you, Simon
son of Jonah, for this was not revealed to you by flesh
and blood, but by my Father in heaven."

Matthew 16:15–17

One afternoon, I sat on my bed contemplating different world religions as well as my own. I began to ask myself why I chose Christianity. Perhaps I was a Christian because of influence—because other people told me Jesus was God's Son. I began to wonder if I could have just as easily been Muslim if I had been raised with that influence. I had been saved for a few years, but that day, I began to question my faith. I asked Jesus to please reveal Himself to me. I wanted to make sure I truly believed in Him for myself so I could raise my children with Christian confidence.

I prayed incessantly and opened my Bible. My eyes fell upon a question in red print: "'Who do people say the Son of Man is?'" (Matthew 16:13). I paused, thinking it was much too coincidental to be an actual coincidence. I continued to read: "'You are the Messiah, the Son of the living God'" (v. 16).

I paused again with my eyes full of tears. *Yes! Yes! You are . . .Christ, Son of the Living God!* I was so amazed and felt so honored that God was communicating with me through His Word. He was *truly* concerned about how I felt and wanted me to be confident in my beliefs. I was so grateful He had led me to those verses and had not punished me for my doubt. Of course, I now know He would never punish me for my doubts, but it was early in my Christian walk, so I didn't know that at the time. At that moment, I discovered He was a loving God Who had heard my prayer and responded through His Word. It was as if He was saying, "It's okay. I do not mind securing your belief in Me."

*Dear Lord, please speak to the hearts of unbelievers who are searching for the "right" religion, so they do not waste another day in uncertainty. Thank You for having patience with me when I had doubts, and thank You for securing my belief in You so I can teach and love others with Christian confidence. Amen.*

# 22

# Handling Disappointment

But seek first his kingdom and his righteousness, and all these things will be given to you as well.

Matthew 6:33

As a Christian, your life is not based on chance, luck, or coincidences. When you follow God obediently and sincerely, He covers you until your last day on earth and into eternity. However, your Christian walk will not exclude you from disappointment. Disappointment is a reality in everyone's life, saved or unsaved, but do not be discouraged. God still has a plan for you.

Both negative and positive situations can prepare you for divine destiny. For example, my son applied to the University of Pennsylvania when he was a senior in high school. He maintained honor roll throughout high school, was involved in several clubs, performed many community service hours, and received many awards. It seemed he was well qualified for the University of Pennsylvania, but he was not accepted.

So, what happened? He concluded that he was destined to be at another institution. However, he didn't fully understand it until he had completed his second year at Rutgers-Camden. He was on the dean's list every semester and received recognition and awards from Rutgers, the state, and local organizations for helping disadvantaged people in the surrounding community. He was truly happy and got so much joy out of helping the residents of Camden that he believed the state school was a divine selection and the Ivy League school, a divine rejection. Could he have gone to the University of Pennsylvania and done the same? No human knows for sure, but the important issue is that my son's first responsibility was to God's kingdom. As a result, God stayed with him and blessed his endeavors.

Like my son, many people want to go to the best school, get the best job, and just have the best of everything. There is nothing wrong with setting goals and having high expectations, but if things don't work out according to your plans, remember God can bless you anywhere. Just because an institution or occupation has an esteemed reputation, that does not necessarily mean you are supposed to be there. Remember, God wants you in the place that is best for *you*. It may not be the most popular place in the world, and it may not be the most attractive position, but if God ordained it, it is for you.

> *Dear Lord, please lead me into Godly purpose. Choose my job, my neighborhood, and my friends. I welcome Your process of divine elimination. I appreciate Your choosing all that is best for me. Amen.*

# 23

# Give Something Away

If anyone has material possessions and sees a brother or
sister in need but has no pity on them, how can the love
of God be in that person? Dear children, let us not love
with words or speech but with actions and in truth.

1 John 3:17–18

Do you have something to give away that someone else can
use? If the answer is yes, give it to them today. Maybe you
feel awkward giving and they feel awkward receiving. There
is a solution for the discomfort you both feel: give more often.
Once you establish the reputation as a giver, people will not feel
uncomfortable receiving from you. Otherwise, they may think
you are giving out of boastfulness. You want it to be clear that
you are giving out of love, so give sincerely and consistently. For
example, if you give pies to your neighbors during the holiday
season, they will not think it strange for you to give them something any other time of the year because you will have set a prec-
edent of giving.

Once you set a standard of giving in an environment, it becomes contagious. Someone else will want to give and so on and
so forth. Not everyone may catch on, but do not be discouraged.

Just continue giving. Then, if someone really has a need and you show up on their doorstep to supply their need, they will not think it uncharacteristic of you.

> *Dear Lord, please continue to put people in my path that I can help. Let them know there is no ulterior motive attached to my gifts. Show them that You are attached to my giving and I only desire to share Your love with them. Amen.*

# 24

# Ripe or Rotten

A good tree cannot bear bad fruit, and a bad tree cannot bear good fruit.

Matthew 7:18

Years ago, my father had a friend who was handsome, articulate, and charismatic. Everyone in the city seemed to admire him with his deep voice and movie star smile. He dressed well, smelled good, and was extremely polite. Even as a child, I admired him.

So when my mother went to the man's home to rescue his wife, Gina, in the middle of the night, I was surprised. He was out of town at the time and was due home in the morning. My mother helped Gina pack her belongings throughout the night. Gina was running away because he had beaten her unmercifully on several occasions. The last time he beat her, she was recovering from a hysterectomy. Prior to that last beating, he had refused to feed her until nine o'clock every night, even though he knew she was too sick to get or prepare her own food. Gina knew she had no choice but to leave. Her escape was successful, and she never returned.

Gina had always tried to give her husband another chance because she loved him. Perhaps she had convinced herself that his good points outweighed his bad ones. After all, he had a good job and was well respected in the community. And he was so kind to people in the street that he seemed to have the capacity to change. But was Gina supposed to stay in a relationship with him and jeopardize her safety? Even though her husband was kind to others, he was *still* an abusive husband. He *produced* rotten fruit.

When you are dealing with people, how they treat *you* is their fruit concerning *you*. When they close the door to the outside world, either ripe or rotten fruit is going to fall. If the fruit is rotten, don't try to peel it, slice it, dice it, and cover it up with pie crust. Just throw it out.

*Dear Lord, please teach me to put as much value on myself as You put on me. Teach me to surround myself with people who sincerely love me and bring forth good fruit. Amen.*

# 25

# One flesh

"For this reason a man will leave his father and mother and be united to his wife, and the two will become one flesh."

Ephesians 5:31

People often ask me how my husband and I have managed to stay successfully married for over two decades. Well, we actually had a rough start. We were both young and neither of us had ever witnessed happy marriages. I, for one, had never seen a man truly love a woman, and I didn't know how to properly respond to my husband's affection, so the first few years were tough. We never hit each other, but we had some fierce arguments. For instance, I used to break dishes, kick over chairs, and swear like a thug. I was afraid he was going to hit me because my father had often hit my mother, so I figured if I acted crazy enough, I would never become a victim.

Then one day my son went to school and told his preschool teacher that his mom and dad fought like "Batman and Robin." My husband and I were both embarrassed, and we talked about how our actions were affecting our son. We both decided we were no longer going to allow our arguments to escalate.

We knew we needed God's guidance. We continued to go to church on Sundays, but we also started to pray together every night. We stopped discussing our problems with other people, and we put each other before everyone else in our lives. We became best friends, wanting nothing but the best for each other, and we became more and more selfless. When I looked at him, I began to see myself, and when he looked at me, he began to see himself. His face became more familiar to me than my own, and my face became more familiar to him than his own. We could not look at each other and knowingly hurt one another because we had truly become one flesh.

*Dear Lord, teach husbands and wives to experience all the joys of marriage by loving each other completely and selflessly. Show them that they can have a successful marriage if they both submit themselves to You first. Amen.*

# 26

# Temples of His Creation

Marriage should be honored by all, and the marriage bed kept pure, for God will judge the adulterer and all the sexually immoral.

Hebrews 13:4

We don't have to compromise our Christian beliefs to fit into a society that promotes sex. It doesn't matter how comfortable we have become with our own lewdness. *God* has no tolerance for it. He created our bodies of sophisticated organs with intricate detail and miraculous functioning for His divine purposes. So, how do you think God feels when humans engage in sexually random practices with temples of His creation? For some, the gender, age, and marital status of their partners don't even matter to them.

For example, incest is too common in our society, and most people are sickened by it. However, we should be sickened by all forms of fornication. Unfortunately, we lowered our basic moral standard as a society long ago, and people have become more comfortable with extreme levels of perversion. We don't seem to know exactly where to draw the line concerning sexual immorality, although the answer is written plainly in God's Word.

The line should be drawn at marriage because that is the only union that is holy and acceptable to Christ. Today and always, we should honor and respect our bodies because we are one of God's wondrous and miraculous creations.

*Dear Lord, please help me make a conscious effort to ward off anything that is offensive to You and make sure I do not become desensitized to the presentation of both subtle and blatant sexual images in our society. Amen.*

# 21

# The Truth

And ye shall know the truth, and the truth shall make you free.

John 8:32 (KJV)

I don't know how many lies I have told in the course of my life-time to maintain "peaceful" relationships. I also can't count the number of times I have sat and smiled and laughed with someone who upset me. That is certainly deception and just as bad as telling a lie. Even though I had good reason to be angry, disappointed, and offended, I simply did not have the courage to speak up. I wanted to preserve my friendships even though I knew they were insincere from the beginning. Since good friends are hard to find, I usually just settled. During my years of settling, I was popular among my peers. I pretended to be exactly who they wanted me to be, but after a while I became uncomfortable compromising my integrity just to keep their company.

After a few years of two such "deceptive relationships," I fi-nally acknowledged the dissonance I was feeling because of it. I began to express my true feelings, and as a result I lost a couple of my closest "friends." I sadly discovered that their love for me was conditional. They were not comfortable with the person I had become once I had fully committed my life to Christ. I understood that relationships require compromise, but I was not going to compromise my relationship with Jesus. Thus, the communication I had with my two friends became less frequent and eventually they stopped calling me. At first, I felt disappointed and rejected, but it all worked out because the time I used to spend talking on the phone with them was replaced by time spent with God.

During my isolation period, I read my Bible more often and wrote over seventy devotions. All of them were revelatory for me because I learned more about myself as I wrote each devotion. While proofreading and revising, I was hit with multiple realities that my subconscious mind was free to release and my conscious mind was finally willing to accept. Everything I had denied and ignored, like my love and resentment toward my father, surfaced and for the first time I allowed myself to feel each emotion without shame. I no longer denied the truth; I was still harboring fear, anger, and pain. However, I also discovered that God gave me just enough humility, courage, and honesty to be used by Him despite my insufficiencies. Knowing these truths gave me the freedom to improve my character and share an important lesson I have learned with others: truth precedes deliverance.

*Dear Lord, thank You for being "the way, the truth, and the life" (John 14:6 KJV). You are the Truth that sets me free, and I appreciate Your sincere friendship. Amen.*

# 28

# A New Language

> But no human being can tame the tongue. It is a restless evil, full of deadly poison.
>
> James 3:8

Summers at Darren's house were unbearable. The fans blew hot air, dust, and strange odors around neglected rooms while Darren and his siblings ate popsicles in front of the television. They watched cartoon after cartoon until their mother came home from work angry, hungry, and too tired to cook. Their mother would walk in the door cursing, holding bags of fast food. However, Darren, the oldest child, was never offended by his mother's language because he had gotten quite used to it.

When Darren became an adult, he accepted Christ in his life and learned a new language. It was not until then that he realized his mother's harsh and bitter words had been injected into his spirit for years. Upon this discovery, Darren did not hold a grudge against his mother. After all, she had sacrificed much of her personal time taking care of her children. Instead, Darren witnessed to his mother and taught her Christ's language of peace.

*Dear Lord, please help me realize that unkind words spoken in a moment can cause years of pain. Please tame my tongue so I can speak Your language of love, peace, and healing. Amen.*

# 29

# I Talk Too Much

Sin is not ended by multiplying words, but the prudent hold their tongues.

Proverbs 10:19

Silence is often undervalued; however, there are times when it holds great value.

I absorb so much when I sit silently in a room. I begin to pay attention to things I usually ignore, like meaningful expressions and body language that are great indications of how someone really feels. I also become more sensitive to people as individuals, no longer treating them like an audience. Most important, I realize that I may learn something valuable by listening to someone else.

On the other hand, incessant talking sometimes disturbs my thoughts because I lose focus in the randomness of conversation. My words become a performance lacking effective communication. At that moment, I should stop and ask myself three questions: What am I saying? What am I hearing? And who am I edifying with my speech?

Sin easily makes its way into petty conversations because the more we talk, the more likely we are to gossip or offend someone; however, if we choose our words wisely, we are less likely to say something inappropriate. We have to remember that Jesus is always in the room. If we could literally see Him there, we would use only a small fraction of the words we typically use. I am sure we would become humbled instantly, becoming a different person—the person who God wants us to be right now. So, today, let us challenge ourselves. Let us remember that Jesus can hear every word that comes out of our mouths, and carefully edit our conversations.

> *Dear Lord, I know I talk too much about nothing sometimes. Please help me edit my conversations today. During this challenge, reveal some things about me that I have not realized before. After today, please give me the strength to face this challenge again tomorrow. Amen.*

# 30

# Control Your Emotions

Get rid of all bitterness, rage and anger, brawling and slander, along with every form of malice.

Ephesians 4:31

You can be angry all day long if you allow yourself to be. There are a number of annoying situations that can potentially set you off every hour of the day. While driving to work, another vehicle might cut you off. When you get to work, you might have to handle a coworker's responsibilities and your own because they called in sick. An unsatisfied client might tell you off on the phone. You might stub your toe on your way over to the water cooler. Then, there might not be any paper cups left when you get there. To top it all off, your boss might be in a bad mood *again*. Then, Smiling Sally tips into the office swinging her white Coach bag and chewing gum like she doesn't have a care in the world.

Individually each of those situations is no big deal, but together they could spoil your whole day. Furthermore, if you allow daily annoyances to ruin enough of your days, you will remain consistently unhappy. However, reading God's Word can help you control your emotions and get through your days peacefully. Tell yourself, "I can do all this through him who gives me strength" (Philippians 4:13). Yes, you can do *everything* through Him, even control your emotions. Then remind yourself that "Fools give full vent to their rage, but the wise bring calm in the end" (Proverbs 29:11). Aren't there enough situations that you absolutely cannot control? Imagine how much more peace you would have in your life if you could just keep *yourself* under control. Remember God promises that you can enjoy "many good days" on earth if you refrain from malicious speech, "turn from evil and do good," and search for peace and follow it (Psalm 34:12–14). According to the Word, peace is something that you have to actively pursue, and consistent prayer and study of the Scriptures can aid you in that pursuit.

> *Dear Lord, I don't want to become angry or annoyed too fast or too often, and I don't want to lie or speak negatively. Please teach me to control myself, and help me in my pursuit of peace. Amen.*

# Expanding Your Album

Love others
unconditionally.

# 31

# Let Love Be Your Goal

If I give all I possess to the poor and give over my body
to hardship that I may boast, but do not have love, I
gain nothing.

1 Corinthians 13:3 (TNIV)

When most people think of the word *love*, a slew of thoughts comes to mind, but most people never come up with their own definition for it. People often say "I love you" too soon, too seldom, or too late. Before you say "I love you," know what you mean. For me, love was selfless and unadulterated concern for others. Before I read God's meaning of love, that was my definition based on more than twenty years' experience as a wife and mother. I love my husband and children purely, unconditionally, and sacrificially.

What do you mean when you say you love someone? Do you love your boss, coworkers, neighbors, family, and friends in the same way? I wish I could say that I do, but only God can love all people so evenly and unreservedly. However, I still welcome you to add love to your list of lifetime goals. To help you in your quest to love, here is the biblical description of love in 1 Corinthians 13:4–7: "Love is patient, love is kind. It does not envy, it does not boast, it is not proud. It does not dishonor others, it is not self-seeking, it is not easily angered, it keeps no record of wrongs. Love does not delight in evil but rejoices with the truth. It always protects, always trusts, always hopes, always perseveres."

Now that you know God's meaning of love, read it a few times with a few people in mind and ask yourself if you love each of them according to the above description. If you do not love them as described by this definition, you may want to reassess your feelings.

> *Dear Lord, teach me how to love according to Your description. Please help me truly love others unconditionally, purely, and profoundly. Amen.*

32

# The Giving Principle

One person gives freely, yet gains even more; another withholds unduly, but comes to poverty. A generous person will prosper; whoever refreshes others will be refreshed.

Proverbs 11:24–25

My Aunt Bev used to say, "The church doesn't have arms and legs to go out and get a job, so the people have to give. That's what they're supposed to do."

The first time I heard Aunt Bev say that, I was in my early twenties. It was a wakeup call for me. I had never thought about how churches get money to help the financially underprivileged members of our society. The church cannot continue to help people in need if no funds are available. How can it continue to give and give and give if people are not consistently making contributions? If all of its members were obedient, the church would never have to think of creative ways to finance its ministries. Unfortunately, that is not the case, and the church has to continue to do God's work even in the midst of its members' disobedience.

We know how difficult life is for many people. Through the Internet and television alone, we witness people suffering around the world. People are sick, hungry, lost, homeless, incarcerated, lonely, addicted, heartbroken, and abused. We know this. Evidence of it surrounds us, yet some of us still have to be *asked* to give.

Some people you never have to ask. Aunt Bev was one of those people. She tithed faithfully and gave freely of herself in and out of church. She lived a good life and died a peaceful death. When family cleaned her house after her death, she had money under her mattress, in sock drawers, under couch pillows, and in other odd places—just hundreds of dollars lying around as freely as dust. Besides this, she left land, property, and money to her children and grandchildren. Sounds like a wealthy woman, huh? Well, Aunt Bev cleaned houses for a living and had been retired for years, living on a fixed income. She made a lot less money than most of us, but she had so much more than many of us.

*Dear Lord, touch the congregations around the globe and make them more sensitive to the needs of others so the church can give happily and freely without financial strain. Also, could You please touch me personally? Let me know if I am withholding anything I should be giving away. Whether it is time, money, or talent, Lord, I want to release it for Your glory. Amen.*

# 33

# Fruits of Your Labor

And if you spend yourselves in behalf of the hungry and satisfy the needs of the oppressed, . . . the Lord will guide you always; he will satisfy your needs in a sun-scorched land and will strengthen your frame. You will be like a well-watered garden, like a spring whose waters never fail.

Isaiah 58:10–11

When I lived in the inner city, both my marriage and my children were young. We had not amassed any wealth, and we lived from paycheck to paycheck for a time; however, we continued to help people who were less fortunate. We did not reach out to others to gain any great reward from God or heaven. Honestly, at the time it just felt like the right thing to do.

There was one person we helped whom I will never forget. We called her "The Bag Lady" as if it were her birth name. We later found out her name was Mattee. The first time we saw Mattee, my three-year-old son and I were sitting on the front porch. She was moving slowly down the walk, overdressed for ninety-plus degree weather. We asked her if she wanted some water. From that day forward, we gave her water every day for the rest of the summer. Eventually, the water turned to fresh fruit, and the fresh fruit to leftover dinner from the night before.

Years later, when my son was a freshman in college, he had to write a paper on something memorable from his childhood. He wrote about Mattee and how he used to hand her plastic bags full of fruit. I was so touched when I read his paper because I started thinking about all the people's lives we had touched when we had very little ourselves and how helping other people made my children more compassionate. I thought about where we were then and where we are now. I thought about how God has moved in our daily lives over the years and how much my children love and respect the Lord and all His creations.

I get so filled with great emotion when I think about how faithful God has been to us. We had no idea He was going to give us so much more than we had given other people. I am glad we didn't know, because a selfish part of us may have been tempted to give Mattee three meals a day instead of one, thinking about all that we were going to get back from God. How sad it would be to give just to get a blessing from God. God knows our hearts, so when you feed the hungry, give money to the poor, or talk to someone who is hurting, do it selflessly. However, if you do not have compassion for those who have less than you have, ask God to teach you how to love outside yourself.

*Dear Lord, I am so appreciative of Your daily presence in my life. Please continue to put people in my path that I can bless. Give me someone to love outside myself today, and continually use me to reflect Your glory. Amen.*

# 34

# Selfless Acts

*. . . Freely you have received; freely give.*

Matthew 10:8

One day, I decided to walk my elderly neighbor's dog, Sweetie, for her because there was snow and ice on the ground. Miss Lena, my neighbor, handed me the leash and a plastic bag to pick up Sweetie's waste. Sweetie and I proceeded down the walk, and I was surprised to see her hobble on three legs. Miss Lena called out the door, "If she has a seizure, just pick her up and hold her till it passes!"

*Honestly,* I thought, *this is much more than I bargained for, walking on ice with a crippled dog that may poop and have a seizure.* It was a very long walk around the block, but when I got back to Miss Lena's house, it was worth it. She was so grateful I had taken Sweetie for a walk. Usually, Sweetie doesn't walk any farther than Miss Lena's front lawn, and it was obvious that Sweetie was excited to go for a longer walk. She bounced happily, leading me around the corner. Looking back on it, it didn't take much of my time or energy, and it meant so much to Miss Lena and Sweetie.

Every day God does things that mean so much to us without ever asking Himself, "What's in it for Me?" Yet, how many selfless acts do we perform on a weekly, monthly, or yearly basis? If we blessed someone for each of God's acts of love toward us, it would take innumerable lifetimes. We could never repay God for all He has done for us, and we could never match His greatness, but we can reflect His nature by helping others freely.

> *Dear Lord, please teach me to perform selfless acts every day. Teach me the eternal value of helping someone else other than myself. Amen.*

# 35

# Unlimited Prayer

Therefore confess your sins to each other and pray for each other so that you may be healed. The prayer of a righteous person is powerful and effective.

James 5:16

A friend of mine called me last week. I thought she just wanted to chat since we had not spoken in a while. She asked me to pray for her niece who was in the hospital. She said, "I know you pray and stuff like that, so could you *please* pray for my niece?"

I told her I would, and I prayed as soon as we hung up. I called her a few days later and left a message on her voicemail, telling her I was still praying for her niece and I had just called to see how she and her family were doing.

Today, I want to encourage you to pray for people outside your circle, and if it is possible follow up your prayer with an email, phone call, or card. People need to know you care about them. In addition to this, pray for people you may never meet. Pray for the homeless woman you speed by on the roadway. Pray for the gentleman next to you at the red light even if he is driving a Porsche and wearing a Rolex watch; he needs prayer too. Pray for the prostitute on the corner; it is only by the grace of God you are not on the corner somewhere selling yourself to survive. Pray for the girl crying and talking to herself in the psych ward; you might be only a situation away from being committed. Pray for the junkie in the alleyway; she is somebody's child. Pray for the stockbroker and the baker. Pray for the chiropractor and the preacher. Pray for the victim and the perpetrator. Pray for the smoker and the gambler. They all need prayer. Pray for the drunkard; he is *your* brother. Pray for the stripper; she is *your* sister. They are *all* our brothers and sisters, mothers and fathers, and sons and daughters. They are all prospective members of the household of faith. Pray for their salvation. Pray for their deliverance.

*Dear Lord, give me the dedicated and selfless mindset I need to improve my prayer life, and please help me find at least one stranger a day to add to my prayer list. Lastly, please give me the love and compassion I need to pray vehemently for Your children. Amen.*

# Unbelievers to Believers

"Whoever belongs to God hears what God says. The reason
you do not hear is that you do not belong to God."

John 8:47

**W**hen I first read John 8:47, I thought, *Now that doesn't make
any sense to me. If unbelievers don't hear Him, then how do they
ever get to the point where they start to hear Him and believe?* Well, I
thought about the first time I was introduced to God's Word. My
mother and I used to read the Bible together when I was a child.
At night, we would read Psalm 23 and recite The Lord's Prayer.
When we got to "Give us this day our daily bread," I used to say
"jelly bread" and fall out laughing as my mother tried to finish
reading. After about two rounds of laughter, we would complete
the prayer.

Although I did not understand the magnitude of the time
spent reading the Bible with my mother, my introduction to
God's Word was positive. My mother and I did not go to church
together, but God's Word was a part of our lives. So, in the fu-
ture when someone approached me about accepting Christ as
my Lord and Savior, it didn't feel too strange for me to follow.
I was stubborn and skeptical, but thankfully the seed had been

planted early in my childhood. This is not the case for everyone, though. Each person's exposure to Christianity is different. Some have had a lot of exposure, others have had little, and some have had none at all. Also, some may have had negative experiences with Christians, so when you speak to unbelievers, you have to be sensitive to their religious histories. You cannot expect them to hear and respond to God's Word in the same way you do, and you cannot expect them to believe in Christ because *you* say He is real. So, how will they ever become believers?

Some become believers or remain unbelievers by watching you. Ask yourself a few questions: Do you exhibit Christlike qualities? Are you loving, patient, and merciful? You do not have to be perfect, but people should, at the very least, enjoy being in your company. You have to remember that you are an active doer of God's Word, so even if unbelievers do not hear God, they can see Him working through you.

> *Dear Lord, speak to the hearts of those who do not know You. If there is anything about me that does not honor You, bring it to my attention and remove it from my character. I do not want it to be a part of my life if it disrupts my relationship with You and others who may or may not know You. Amen.*

# 31

# Judge Not

"Do not judge, or you too will be judged."

Matthew 7:1

A cashier at our neighborhood market had such an unwelcoming disposition that I would avoid her checkout line. Sometimes she would be the only cashier working and I, of course, would have to get in her line. I would smile and say good morning as pleasantly as I knew how without breaking into song and dance. She would respond with a mumbled hi. After that, she would work in silence, and I would bag my groceries and pay in silence.

One day my husband and I were shopping in that same neighborhood grocery store. I told him not to go to the "evil cashier." Of course he carefully angled the cart between the candy bar and magazine racks of her aisle. He asked her about her holiday and talked about the weather. Meanwhile, I was thinking, *He is so corny, and this is so unnecessary.* He called her by the name displayed on her nametag. She mumbled and grumbled for a while, but he kept on talking to her.

Then she held up my frozen macaroni and cheese and said, "You should make it from scratch." I looked at her strangely. Then she gave me advice on how to prepare the best macaroni and cheese. "You gotta use that cheese from behind the meat counter. Tell them it's for mac and cheese. They'll know what you're talkin' about."

My husband said, "How about we just come to your house and eat?"

She smiled and said, "Anytime. I haven't had much company since my son passed away last year."

My husband and I did not go to her home, but every time we saw her in the market, she smiled, talked, and laughed as she ran our items across the scanner.

*Dear Lord, I am sorry for judging others. Please remind me that everyone has a story that I may not know or understand. Please forgive me and fill my heart with compassion for everyone I meet. Amen.*

# 38

# Love Every Member

Be completely humble and gentle; be patient, bearing with one another in love.

Ephesians 4:2

A decade ago I had decided I was not going to join another church. I had been an unhappy member of two churches in the past, and I no longer saw the purpose of having a church home. Church members did not act the way I expected them to act, and I was severely disappointed. I honestly thought everyone would be on their best behavior in the body of Christ. Well, my naivety left me in a strange place. I kept thinking, *What is wrong with these people?* I was getting disgusted left and right.

Now, mind you, out in the world, I had so much tolerance for people. I could think of an excuse for anyone who acted up. If someone out in the street committed a horrible crime, I would be the first to say, "Now you never know what kind of childhood that person had" or "You don't know what that person has to go through on a day to day basis." However, when I joined the church, I became someone else. I still had tolerance for worldly folks, but as far as church folks were concerned, I was not try-ing to give them any excuses. Whenever they acted ungodly, a siren would go off in my head, and I would overreact to their faults, allowing no room for human frailty in the body of Christ. No room.

Now, how did I get out of this? Well, to tell you the truth, I am still partially in it. Every now and then I still need a reminder from the Lord. However, I'll tell you how I got better. God slowly made me aware of my own imperfections, and He was so subtle and loving with His presentation of my faults that I felt ashamed I had judged my Christian family so harshly.

Once you allow yourself the freedom to love every member of your church family unconditionally, you improve your Christian experience. Can you imagine what power the church would have if each member of the congregation decided to love one another wholeheartedly? This may not be an easy feat because we are all human, but if we willfully decided to love others as much as Christ loves us all, the church would be a more welcoming institution. We must remember that we are one body, and every part of the body needs care. Every part needs to feel the love and support of the entire church family.

*Dear Lord, teach me to love every member of my church family unreservedly. Please help me become a more productive and less critical member of Your house of worship. Amen.*

# 39

# Pray for Wisdom

"So give your servant a discerning heart to govern your people and to distinguish between right and wrong. For who is able to govern this great people of yours?"

1 Kings 3:9

God came to Solomon in a dream and asked him what he wanted. King Solomon asked for wisdom and understanding. God was moved by Solomon's answer because he did not ask God to extend his life, kill his enemies, or make him wealthy. God answered the king's humble prayer and gave Solomon "a wise and discerning heart." However, God also gave Solomon wealth, honor, and a long life (1 Kings 3:5–14).

If God were to give you a kingdom today, would you be able to rule it successfully? Likewise, if God made you president of a company, would you know how to run it and handle the questions and concerns of your clients and employees? You need wisdom and understanding to be a great leader.

Materially, if God gave you houses, cars, and land, would you be able to maintain it all? Similarly, if God gave you an extra five dollars, would you know how to save it, turn it over, and increase it? You also need wisdom and understanding to handle material wealth.

Physically, if God gave you two hundred years to live, would you take better care of your body, knowing it would have to sustain you through two centuries? More realistically, do you take care of your body now? You need wisdom and understanding to take care of your physical health as well.

We want so much from God. However, we must remember, "From everyone who has been given much, much will be demanded; and from the one who has been entrusted with much, much more will be asked" (Luke 12:48). You need wisdom and understanding for all that you ask. You need it for you and the people who are going to come to you for guidance and advice. Finally, you need wisdom and understanding that can be passed down and continued through generations.

*Dear Lord, please give me wisdom and understanding today that I can pass on to others. No matter how many years I have on earth, I want to be effective. I want to honor You with all You have given me. Teach me that it does not matter if it seems like a whole lot to others and a little to some. Teach me that there is great power and significance in small and large things, both material and immaterial. Please make me more sensitive to the purpose and significance of everything You created, and give me the wisdom and understanding to take care of it all. Amen.*

40

# Everyone Is Required to Help

The Lord is a refuge for the oppressed, a stronghold in
times of trouble. Those who know your name trust in you,
for you, Lord, have never forsaken those who seek you.

Psalm 9:9–10

I think one of the toughest things about life is watching others
suffer. There is so much hate and pain in the world that it is
too overwhelming for our minds to conceive. On every conti-
nent on the globe you can find someone sadder, hungrier, sicker,
or lonelier than you. From the boy soldiers in Africa to the or-
phans of Asia, from the sweatshops of Europe to the inner cities
of North America, there are innumerable people tormented every
day. We cannot even begin to fathom the degree to which our
fellow humans are suffering, and unfortunately, the suffering does
not end with the human population. Animals across the globe are
suffering too. Millions of God's creatures are living and dying
under intolerable conditions. Yes, "the Lord is a refuge" (Psalm
9:9), but where do you fit in this world of suffering? Why are you
here, and what is your contribution to the oppressed?

You can help by making sure you are not the cause or the op-
pressor, spreading God's free gift of love, and helping others on

a consistent basis. Everyone who is able to help is called to help. Now, you may not be gifted to help in the same way as someone else, but you do have a divine purpose to help someone other than yourself.

I will use my children as an example. My son loves people. At the age of twenty he started Miracles Global, Inc., a non-profit organization that helps sick and disadvantaged people. My daughter, on the other hand, loves animals. She is a vegan and volunteers at a no-kill animal shelter in South Jersey. They are both from the same parents, raised with the same morals and values, but called to help in different ways. Not everyone is gifted to work with children as my son is, and I am telling you, not everyone is cut out to chip frozen poop off dog runs in winter as my daughter does. However, God wants you helping somewhere in the world. I don't know if it is just around the corner from you or across the globe, but you have a responsibility to make the world a better place.

*Dear Lord, I pray that I am not responsible for any pain or sadness on earth. If I am, please bring it to my attention so I can change my ways. Please help me become a more empathetic and compassionate person so I can improve the lives of thousands. Amen.*

# When the Picture fades

PLant and water
for the next
generation.

41

# Think on Eternal Life

Even though I walk through the darkest valley, I will fear
no evil, for you are with me; your rod and your staff, they
comfort me.

Psalm 23:4

Shortly before my paternal grandfather died, he said, "Don't
worry about me. I'm a winner if I live or if I die."

I often think of how strong my grandfather was when facing death and how secure he was in his Christian beliefs. I pray
I can be as strong and as faithful in my last days on earth. In the
meantime, I try to give each day my best and not think pessi-
mistically about death.

Quite honestly, many people prefer not to think about death,
but every now and then it crosses some of our minds with a cloak
of anxiety. It cannot speak. It cannot hear. It does not walk. It
does not move in a human sense, yet it frightens some of us because, although it is often categorized with peace, it is final and
it is certain. So, how do we live joyfully and peacefully on earth
with death prowling around our lives?

We have to remember that heaven is also final and certain,
and God promises eternal life to those who accept Jesus Christ

as their Lord and Savior (John 3:16). Jesus will be there with you when you take your last breath, and you will feel the divine impact of His love on your spirit as He leads you to heaven. Flesh makes you sad and afraid, but you have nothing to fear if you have fully committed your life to Christ. God orders your life until your final moment on earth, and after you have fulfilled your purpose here, you will live eternally with Jesus. He is a God Who is with you in life and in death, so you are truly a winner if you live or if you die.

> *Dear Lord, I desire to worship You for an eternity, but I must admit that I am sometimes afraid of death. Please get rid of my fears and allow me to enjoy every moment of my life. Teach me to focus on Your perfect and divine love that is available to me now and forever. Amen.*

# 42

# Thank God for Preservation

You are my hiding place; you will protect me from trouble
and surround me with songs of deliverance.

Psalm 32:7

In the early eighties, I was a member of a dance company. We
spent a lot of time rehearsing at the studio and performing at
various locations. After I resigned from the company, three of
the dancers died of AIDS. I got very anxious thinking about my
own mortality. I thought, *They were young and died, and I could
die too.* I had never thought of death so seriously or prayed so
vehemently.

I thought back on our dance routines, and one stood out
more than the rest. It was a routine we performed in a play called
*Yes, God Is Real.* We were devils in the play, dancing in red cos-
tumes with smoke surrounding us. I was touched every time I
sat backstage, waiting for my cue and listening intently to the
rest of the cast sing gospel songs. I was moved by their words,
and I believed what they said because they sang each song with
so much passion. Little did I know, my young, carnal mind was
being transformed.

God used *Yes, God Is Real* to put songs in my memory that I sang throughout the difficult years that followed. He also preserved me during the times I was not thinking of Him, the times I was preoccupied with sin. I am still here, and I do not take my life for granted. I am grateful for His protection. I am also at peace knowing I am redeemed by His blood (Ephesians 1:7) and saved from the fires of hell. Equally, when Jesus hung on the cross, He did the same thing for you, so praise His name. Sing songs of deliverance and thank Him for His preservation.

*Dear Lord, thank You for preserving me. Humble me daily as I deliver Your message to everyone who needs to make it through another day in a life that is not always easy. Thank You for protecting me on earth, and thank You for the eternal preservation of my spirit. Amen.*

# 43

# My father, My father

Blessed are those who mourn, for they will be comforted.

Matthew 5:4

When I was seventeen years old, I sat in my bedroom thinking about my biological father. I had not seen him in seven years, but for some reason, on that particular day, I became overwhelmed by emotions and flashbacks of time spent with him. I walked in my mother's bedroom and fell on the bed crying, releasing feelings I had suppressed.

"I want my father," I cried like I was still ten years old, waiting for him on the front step.

After a brief search, I found him in Leesburg State Prison with a six-year sentence. For his remaining years of incarceration, I visited him regularly, and we talked on the phone extensively. He shared stories of his tragic past and ongoing struggle with a heroin addiction. We talked about God, and he told me how he would hide his Bible from the other inmates as he walked across the open field of the minimum security prison.

When he was released, we spent less time together than when he was incarcerated. I began to worry. Then, in the middle of the afternoon, I heard a small knock on my front door. It was my father. He looked much thinner than he had before. I let him in. Humbly, he asked me if I would pray with him because he felt himself "slipping back." He confessed that he had drunk some alcohol and a bottle of cough medicine. I remember thinking, *At least it's not heroin.* He lightly yanked my hand, pulling me slowly down to my knees. He prayed fervently to the Lord. When he left, I just knew he would be all right. Shockingly, less than a year later, he died of a heroin overdose.

I became angry, guilt-ridden, and depressed. I kept thinking, *My father and I prayed together, and he still died.* I just did not understand, and I did not want to go to church anymore because the last thing I wanted to hear from people was, "God won't put more on you than you can bear." Then, I dreamed my father came to me and told me to keep my family in church. The dream seemed so real that I figured it was a message from the Lord.

My family and I kept going to church, and eventually I learned that you don't have to understand everything to have a relationship with God. You are going to be disappointed sometimes, and people you love are going to die. People have been dying long before you were born, but when it becomes personal, you are more likely to change your perception of God and walk away from Him. Today, I am telling you to stay with Him, and if you don't know Him, find out Who He is by consistently praying and reading His Word. When I found God, I realized that *He* was the father I was crying for in my mother's bedroom.

*Dear Lord, help me realize that life on earth is not supposed to be perfect, but You remain perfect even in the face of tragedy. I love You, Lord, and I am going to follow You, no matter what each day brings. Thank You for loving me, and thank You for bringing me through. Amen.*

# 44

# Seeds Still Grow

The one who plants and the one who waters have one purpose, and they will each be rewarded according to their own labor.

1 Corinthians 3:8

When my forty-one-year-old dad died horrifically from a heroin overdose, I started to feel a little less comfortable in the world. I began to anticipate bad news and fear the worst from most situations. I realized, then, that I had to deal with my father's death because it had jumpstarted a series of negative thoughts and emotions in me.

First I had to understand why his death bothered me so much. He had been in and out of my life, so I never expected to be as upset as I was when he died. However, he and I had gotten closer as I got to know him better. He told me the grim details of his childhood and the unbelievable struggles he had in adulthood. His mother ran a brothel from her home, and his job as a child was to change the sheets in between clients. His mother also beat him over the head with iron skillets and ordered him to clean up blood after she stabbed a man in their living room. He was an alcoholic by the time he was twelve and a heroin addict by the time he was seventeen.

After hearing my dad's story, I understood how this man, who was smart, charming, and creative, had become a substance abuser. However, he was not just a substance abuser. He was an excellent writer and an avid reader. He was intelligent enough to become a successful author, businessman, or lawyer and certainly comical enough to star in his own sitcom. I saw so many possibilities in him, and when he died, so did those possibilities. For a long time, his death took away my hope and my faith, and I had to figure out how I was going to deal with the irreversible loss.

I dealt with the loss by focusing on the family he had left behind. He had children and grandchildren who were still young and full of possibilities. It made me realize that I had to stop mourning over who my father could have been; I could not go back and cure his drug addiction, nor could I bring him back to life, but I could continue living and giving the best of myself to everyone I was responsible for, especially my own children. I could also focus less on the loss of my earthly father and focus more on my Heavenly Father's grace. With Jesus, I could. And thank God, I did. I regained my hope.

If someone you love has died, you can regain your hope too. There are so many people you must continue to express your love and concern for on earth. Although people pass on, seeds still grow. God needs you to plant and water for the next generation.

*Dear Lord, thank You for making possibilities realities in the lives of my family and friends who have experienced the loss of a loved one. Please give me the time and compassion I need to continue to care for the living, and the faith to know that You are taking care of my loved ones who have gone to heaven. Amen.*

# 45

# Man Cannot Kill the Soul

"Do not be afraid of those who kill the body but cannot kill the soul. Rather, be afraid of the One who can destroy both soul and body in hell."

Matthew 10:28

My close friend moved from the East Coast to the West Coast. Over the years, we kept in touch by phone, email, and snail mail. She used to send me photographs of herself and her husband, and I used to send her pictures of my children. Whenever we talked, we shared the pains and joys of our separate lives. She was sad she never had children, but I assured her that "you are blessed if you have them and blessed if you don't." We got a good laugh out of that just like we did with all things. Every time we talked, we laughed most of the time, regardless of what was going on in our lives.

I called her again one day, but her phone was disconnected. I sent her a letter, a picture, and an email, but I received no response. I became discouraged because I had no way of contacting her. We were not from the same hometown. We did not have any friends in common, and I had only met her parents once when we were teenagers. Then one day I was cleaning out the drawer of my nightstand. I found the last letter she had written me. As always, there was a photo enclosed. I stared at the photo and felt that Judy had died. Then, I remembered I had asked her for her mother's number shortly before Judy had moved out West. I searched for my old phonebook and found her mother's number.

I spoke to her mother a long while, and I tried to listen and concentrate between sobs as my dreadful premonition was confirmed. Judy had been dead for two years. The last time I spoke to her was a couple months before her death. She was murdered by her husband—the man who had smiled at me through several photographs. I could not come to terms with it. I cried every day for two weeks. I wrote to relieve the pain, completing a sonnet I had written in her memory.

Eventually, I started thinking more optimistically. Matthew 10:28 reminded me that her husband had no authority over her eternal life. He had not destroyed her soul. Then, I remembered the last phone conversation I had had with Judy. We were talking about the Lord, and she was just as excited about God as I was, commenting, "Amen," and "I know that's right," whenever I talked about God's goodness. So now, whenever I get sad about her death, I think of Matthew 10:28 and my last conversation with Judy, and it gives me peace in place of mourning.

*Dear Lord, life is rough sometimes, and murder is hard to deal with, but You are always there to comfort me. Thank You for reminding me that man has no authority over the soul. I am so grateful that You have the final say on where we spend eternity. Amen.*

46

# Move on Despite Tragedy

When the perishable has been clothed with the imperishable, and the mortal with immortality, then the saying that is written will come true: "Death has been swallowed up in victory."

1 Corinthians 15:54

My grandmother held three jobs. She worked fulltime at a nursing home in Atlantic City, part-time as a waitress at a local restaurant, and part-time as a home health aide. Although my grandmother was in her early forties, she had just become fully independent. She had enrolled in evening classes to obtain her G.E.D., got her driver's license, and purchased a used car. Unfortunately, she and my grandfather were legally separated, and with five older children, she was finally able to concentrate on herself.

My grandmother started dating Jerry, a bellhop who worked at the restaurant's adjoining hotel. He was twenty years her senior and claimed that he too was separated from his spouse. When my grandmother discovered he was still living with his wife, she ended their relationship. Jerry threatened and stalked my grandmother for days. However, no one took his actions seriously, until my mother received a phone call from the restaurant.

"Jerry just shot your mother up!" It was the voice of the sixteen-year-old waitress who worked at the restaurant with my grandmother. The young waitress later told police that Jerry came in the back door of the establishment and shot my grandmother three times before shooting himself. Later, my mother had to identify her mother's body at the Atlantic City Medical Center. The residual effects of that tragedy affected our family for a couple generations. When I would complain about small things, my mother would say, "Look, my mother was murdered! Save your energy for the big stuff." As much as I wanted to ask what that had to do with anything, I knew better, and I later learned that it had a lot to do with everything.

As I got older, some of that "big stuff" came just as my mother had promised. Sometimes I felt like I was hit coming and going, but I knew I *had* to keep going. "Big stuff" will come your way too, but you have to move past it all just like my grandmother's five children did. From watching them, I learned that death and tragedy are not excuses to give up on life and certainly not excuses to give up on God. All five of them were survivors, and no matter what comes your way, you have to be a survivor too.

*Dear Lord, I am so grateful for Your divine strength that helps me cope in a world that can be frightening and unpredictable. During times of mourning, thank You for reminding me of Your gift of everlasting life. It is this gift that keeps me hopeful in the face of death. Amen.*

# 47

# "The Day I Started Living"

"Do not let your hearts be troubled. You believe in God; believe also in me. My Father's house has many rooms; if that were not so, would I have told you that I am going there to prepare a place for you? And if I go and prepare a place for you, I will come back and take you to be with me that you also may be where I am. You know the way to the place where I am going."

John 14:1–4

My mother is not sure what came first—the hives or the convulsions. The doctor gave her a shot of penicillin. Her body convulsed. Shoes flew off her feet. Hives closed off her airway. She scratched at her neck, trying to make a hole to breathe. As one of the nurses said, "Oh my God, Doctor, she's dying," my mother watched her own hand turn gray and stiffen.

A doctor and nurses tried to restore my mother's breathing. As she watched from the ceiling, she thought comically, "Wow, they're really working hard to bring me back." Next, there was nothing but darkness. Then, there was a brilliant light, a light so brilliant she could not see the man's face who had on a robe with his arms outstretched. He showed her everything she had done wrong in her life. My grandmother, who had died five years prior, was there also, speaking in my mother's defense, reminding him of all the good her daughter had done.

My mother was active in her community, helping the under-privileged even though she *was* the underprivileged. She volun-teered for Welfare Rights, Narcotic Addicts Recovery Center, and the Community Development Block Grant Program. She sat on several boards and was also a mother, struggling to raise a child in the projects.

My mother pleaded with the man, whom she now refers to as Jesus. "I can't die now. I would stay here with you, but I have an eight-year-old daughter, and she doesn't have anyone but me. She is just not ready for this."

The man spoke calmly in the most beautiful voice my mother had ever heard. "Rhonda, scream. Just scream."

My mother tried to scream. It was very difficult at first, but once she was able to get a bit of sound out, she saw a glimpse of the room where her earthly body lay. Whenever she would stop screaming, there would be darkness. The longer she screamed, the longer she saw the light of the room, so she began to scream uncontrollably. The doctor and nurses tried to calm her down, explaining that they had just given her a shot of adrenalin. Re-garding her return, my mother has often said, "They think they brought me back, but it wasn't them."

After that ordeal, my mother just wanted to get home to make sure I was okay, but the doctor called an ambulance to transport her to the hospital. Meanwhile, I was home worried because she had not come home from work. My uncle picked me up and took me to the hospital to see her. When I got there, she was sitting in a wooden wheelchair, looking exhausted with bloody scratches on her neck. I asked her what happened. She grabbed my hands, looked into my eyes, and said the most meaningful thing I have ever heard her say. She enunciated each word slowly and sincerely. "Shawn, don't you *ever* ask me again if there is a God, because *there is* a God."

Prior to that day, which was October 8, 1976, I had often asked my mother, "Is there a God? Is God real?" One day she answered, "No. I don't know, Shawn. When you die, you just go in the ground." Yet she continued to read The Lord's Prayer to me every night before bed, so I wasn't fully convinced. Well, after October 8, 1976, I was fully convinced that *there was* a God, and I never asked her again.

My mother says, "October 8, 1976 is the day I started living." Psychiatrists tried to convince her that she had imagined the whole incident, and others said it didn't make sense biblically. Regardless of what others have to say about the validity of my mother's story, the incident changed her life for the better. She became even more helpful in her community. She sent me to Sunday school, and she began to appreciate things on earth like grass, trees, and even concrete. For the first time, she could truly see the miracles on earth *and* look forward to spending eternity with Jesus.

*Dear Lord, You have decorated heaven and earth with Your magnificent glory, divine creativity, and awesomeness, and I am so grateful that You have blessed me with the opportunity to enjoy both heaven and earth. Amen.*

48

# Jesus Is the Root

"The grass withers and the flowers fall, but the word of
our God endures forever."

Isaiah 40:8

My husband treated our lawn like it was a piece of fine art.
Every time I looked at it, I smiled. People complimented
us on it as they walked by, and drivers admired it from their car
windows. It was healthy, green, and immaculate through *every*
season. Then one year, fungus spread throughout its blades. Hundreds of strange little flying bugs hovered over its surface, and
clumps of grass separated from their roots like cheap toupees.
Looking at it grossed me out, so I would walk quickly from my
car with my shoulders scrunched, eyes squinted, and face twisted.
Needless to say, I refused to touch it.

I mourned each blade from afar as my husband examined each
patch. After all, the grass was *his* baby; however, I questioned him
about it repeatedly until he gave it "sufficient" time and attention. He worked on it a long time too, but our grass never fully
recovered. My husband and I finally stopped worrying about it,
once we realized worrying was not doing any good. We didn't
neglect it, but we didn't obsess over it either. We continued to

do our part, making sure it was properly watered and nurtured, but we left the rest of its care to God.

Once you do your part, leave the rest to God. There is nothing else you can do. Diseased grass is a lighthearted example, but there are many situations in your life that can cause you to separate from your roots, and you have no idea how or if you should reconnect. You are not sure if you should move forward on your own or depend on the only support system you are accustomed to. All you know is that you feel unstable, and your friends and family seem just as unstable as you are. Well, their foundation may be shaky because they are not grounded in God's Word (Matthew 7:24–27), and they may not be able to help you because they cannot help themselves. If this is the case, and you feel like everything around you seems to be withering and dying away, read God's Word and apply it to your life. It will give you endurance, and you will be able to stand in the midst of your circumstances because Jesus is "the Root" (Revelation 22:16) Who will keep you grounded for eternity.

*Dear Jesus, You said, "Heaven and earth will pass away, but my words will never pass away" (Matthew 24:35). I trust You and I trust Your Word. All the issues, concerns, and details of my life will have to follow You obediently. Every problem and situation will have to respond to Your Word and live in the midst of Your glory. You are the love of my life, my Heavenly Father, and my Healer. I honor You, Lord. I worship You, and I trust You with my life. Amen.*

# 49

# Sufficient Grace

... "My grace is sufficient for you, for my power is made perfect in weakness."

2 Corinthians 12:9a

My Uncle Joe was a United States Army Veteran who served during the Vietnam War. Shortly after he returned to the states, his mother was murdered. He also suffered from diabetes and had both legs amputated as a result of the disease, so Uncle Joe was not unfamiliar with tragedy, yet he pressed forward, got married, raised four wonderful children, and enjoyed the balance of his life.

The last few years of his life, Uncle Joe was on dialysis. He endured the process bravely. When he passed away, it was difficult for the family. He was a kind man who gave away time and money to anyone who needed it. At family gatherings, he was the master storyteller, fully animated with tones and facial expressions that made everyone in the room laugh. Unlike with some adults who were preoccupied with their busy lives, children mattered when Uncle Joe was around. When he spoke, he included everyone in the conversation, and he had a childlike honesty that made everyone comfortable in his presence.

A few weeks before Uncle Joe's death, I talked to him about our family history and his life. I wanted to know how a face that had seen so much tragedy could smile so often. I never asked him the question directly. I just listened to him reminisce for hours, and eventually I got my answer. Out of everything he said to me, I remembered one phrase. "The Lord has been good to me all . . . my life," Uncle Joe said, tired and ready to end the call.

Think about how good the Lord has been to you. Even in the midst of all the sadness you have experienced since your birth, God has given you many reasons to smile. Even through the toughest times of your life, God's grace was enough to bring you through. If my uncle could go on with his life, smiling and making others laugh in the midst of his struggles, so can you. Today, make a decision that no matter what, with God on your side, you are going to enjoy your life too.

*Dear Lord, please teach me to recognize that Your power is made perfect in weakness. No matter what goes on in my life, I know You will be there to strengthen me. I appreciate the times You have already held me up after I buckled under emotional pain and kept me up when I could not stand on my own.. Thank You for Your divine strength that continues to sustain me. Lord, You have truly been good to me all my life. Amen.*

# 50

# The World's Troubles

He was despised and rejected by mankind, a man of suffering, and familiar with pain.

Isaiah 53:3a

Yesterday morning, I watched the news. There were stories of one murder after another.

Yesterday afternoon, I looked through my mail and found pictures of missing children.

Yesterday evening, my son told me it was the year anniversary of his friend's death. Needless to say, I did not sleep well at all. Then, at 3:00 a.m., I woke up praying. I could feel God's presence. He knows the world's troubles sometimes consume me. He knows there are days when I am more sensitive than others, days when I internalize the unfairness of war, poverty, genocide, and world hunger. Sometimes I just sit and wonder why so many people are suffering.

I don't get angry at God like I used to because my anger didn't improve the world and it was destroying my personal relationship with Christ. I still feel uncomfortable about things sometimes, though, because I can't explain them, like people murdering innocent people. I know it's because of sin and the depravity of man's heart, but still, I don't fully understand why it has to play out this way. In my lifetime, I have known many people who have lived unhappy lives. I have also seen beautiful people suffer and die young. Then I think of how Jesus suffered for all of us, and that doesn't seem fair to me either. There are just some days when I sit and think, *This just does not make any sense to me at all.*

If you are anything like me, you just have to come to the realization that the world is going to continue to have troubles, and you have to figure out how to live joyously in the midst of it all. Earth is not supposed to be heaven, and you are never going to fully understand why things are the way they are, so you have to consciously decide to make the very best of every day. I know it's not easy, but there are also so many beautiful things and people in the world that still remind you of God's greatness. Yearn to see God's power and glory in these things daily.

*Lord, help me realize that although tough times must come, I have a Savior Who is empathetic to the world's pain because He too has suffered. Please remind me that Jesus has overcome earthly affliction and is there to comfort us always. Amen.*

# Restoring Your Photo

Jesus can restore
your entire life.

# 51

# Respect and Praise

So God created the great creatures of the sea and every living thing with which the water teems and that moves about in it, according to their kinds, and every winged bird according to its kind. And God saw that it was good. God blessed them and said, "Be fruitful and increase in number and fill the water in the seas, and let the birds increase on the earth." And there was evening, and there was morning—the fifth day. And God said, "Let the land produce living creatures according to their kinds: the livestock, the creatures that move along the ground, and the wild animals, each according to its kind." And it was so.

Genesis 1:21–24

We have to restore our perception of time, nature, animals, people, and everything else God created. When we were toddlers, everything was new to us. The details of a human face, a cat's fur, a dog's tail, fingers, toes, sand, mud, water, the sun, and the moon were all objects of our curiosity. Amazed and sometimes awed, we explored God's world with a respect that some of us lose over time. However, God not only deserves our continual respect, He also deserves our continual praise.

How do we allow our praise and respect to diminish when we have no control over day, night, nature, and time and no ability to create any of what we see? God, on the other hand, has both day and night in His possession. Spring, summer, winter, and fall appear when He calls. Even spans of time from milliseconds to eternity are under His command. He is the Father of creatures named and unnamed that swim, creep, and fly across sea, land, and sky. He breathed life into the enormous and the small. The 200-ton, 110-foot blue whale is not too big for God, and the cell, the basic structure of all organisms, is not too small. Even the red-nosed, blue-lined mandrill's face is not too colorful for him, and the white dove's wings are not too plain. Nor is the lion too majestic for our divine King of Kings, the sole Creator of all living things.

We sometimes have to take a second look at God's creation to renew our perspective. If we examine the details of things we see every day, every day becomes a miracle to us. If we concentrate on the fine intricacy of our own bodies, we begin to see ourselves as miracles. If we think on the infinite power God *must* possess to create us and everything else in heaven and on earth, we realize that we are small beings in a universe full of miracles upon miracles upon miracles created by our Heavenly Father, Who deserves our continual respect and praise.

*Dear Heavenly Father, I want to see You in things I normally take for granted. Grass, trees, birds, and people have become so common in my daily life that I sometimes fail to notice You in them. So much has become too familiar to me. Please give me a new perception today—one in which I can marvel at Your creations like a toddler examining the world. Amen.*

# 52

# Give Your Best Every Day

Why, you do not even know what will happen tomorrow. What is your life? You are a mist that appears for a little while and then vanishes. Instead, you ought to say, "If it is the Lord's will, we will live and do this or that."

James 4:14–15

Only God knows the end of human laughter and tears for each one of us, so treat everyone as if you will never see them again. Greet them with love. Treat them with love. Leave them with love. We know for sure that our flesh is mortal, but we do not know the time and place of its expiration.

When you deal with people, give them your best. Give them your best smile, your best handshake, your best words, and your best thoughts. They too are God's creation, and, as with you, God has a special plan and purpose for their lives.

*Dear Lord, teach me not to take Your promise of eternal life for granted. Remind me that I am responsible for how I treat everyone I come in contact with. I am alive today because of You, and if it is Your will, I will wake up tomorrow fully responsible for how I live. Amen.*

# 53

# Choose Unity over Division

If a house is divided against itself, that house cannot stand.

Mark 3:25

Is it fair to hold the church to a higher standard than the world in the presence of ongoing human frailty? Undoubtedly, Christians are humans with many imperfections, but we shouldn't expect them to have the same reaction as people of the world when one of their members falls from grace. Unfortunately, some churchgoers gossip just as much as people who don't go to church. How can a church thrive and provide healing to its members if this person is talking about that person? Each member should be able to trust that their church family sincerely cares about them and has their sincere interests at heart. I know it's a lot to ask, but if each one of us can just start with ourselves, it will make a difference. We have to use our words, written or spoken, to heal and uplift our church family. Although we are human, we want to strive to be examples of Christ.

*Dear Lord, teach me to be a unifier in the body of Christ and a humble edifier in the world so I may demonstrate Your qualities with my actions and words. Amen.*

# 54

# Jesus Truly Loves You

For God so loved the world that he gave his one and
only Son, that whoever believes in him shall not perish
but have eternal life.

John 3:16

Imagine how much Jesus must love us. He *died* for us. Is there anyone you would die for? If you are a parent, you would probably die for your child. If you are a husband or a wife, you would probably die for your spouse. If you can think of anyone in this world you would die for, then you can probably relate to the sacrifice Jesus made for us on the cross. Take the love you have for that special person you would be willing to sacrifice your life for and give it divine magnification! It is a love that is beyond human description. Jesus doesn't care what you look like or where you're from. He doesn't care if you have money or if you're broke. He doesn't care if you graduated from college or just got released from prison. Jesus *truly* loves you, and He sacrificed His life for every single person on earth, including you.

God truly loves you more than anyone else could ever love you. Do you know of anyone in the world who has made a greater sacrifice than Jesus has made for you? "He was pierced for our transgressions, he was crushed for our iniquities; the punishment that brought us peace was on him, and by his wounds we are healed" (Isaiah 53:5). No one else can do that for you! No one else can wash away your sins, heal your body and your mind, restore your strength, and transform your entire life no matter where you came from or who you are. With Him, you don't have to pay a fee, get an advanced degree, or fill out an application. Jesus can restore your entire life for free because He has already paid the price. *He* suffered so you could live. That's how much Jesus loves you!

*Dear Lord, thank You for loving me! I just want to praise You today and every day for Your perfect and merciful love. Please accept my thanks and my sincere praise for all You have done for me. Amen.*

# 55

# The Holy Spirit

After they prayed, the place where they were meeting
was shaken. And they were all filled with the Holy Spirit
and spoke the word of God boldly.

Acts 4:31

Just because *you* haven't experienced something, that doesn't
mean it's not real. It's funny how some folks don't believe something exists because it's out of the realm of their personal experience. For example, some people don't believe in the Holy Spirit
because they have not knowingly experienced His power. I understand that view because I was skeptical before I was touched by
the Holy Spirit. It wasn't expected and I wasn't looking for Him,
but it was the most precious and sacred moment of my life.

It was in the wee hours of the morning. I heard this beautiful
singing. Then, this love entered my heart and spread throughout
my chest. It was the first time I felt pure love physically move in
my body. I have never felt so beautiful inside. I honestly thought
I was dreaming because I had never felt that kind of love. I am
in love with my husband, and I love my children, but there was
something so different about the love I felt that night. For the
first time, I understood how human love is a very small fragment

of God's love. When the sun came up, I had convinced myself that I had imagined the whole experience. The Lord knew He had to confirm for me that it was real because it honestly felt too wonderful to be true.

The next day I went to church in Atlantic City with my family. It was Mother's Day. During the sermon, the minister talked about the Holy Spirit piercing your chest and entering your heart. He described the experience I had the night before. He said it was real and that it "is the love of God, spreading throughout your chest." He described my experience using the same words I was thinking. Now, he was not speaking to me personally; he was speaking to the congregation, but I got my confirmation. Days, months, and years later, more confirmations would follow. The Holy Spirit had become a normal part of my life.

I pray the Holy Spirit will become a normal part of your life too. He is not unreachable, and He is not a scary, fictitious character floating around the earth. The Bible explains that the Holy Spirit is a Counselor Who stays with you and resides in you (John 14:17) and teaches you and reminds "you of everything . . . [Jesus] said" (John 14:26). The Bible also states that "God's love has been poured out into our hearts through the Holy Spirit, who has been given to us" (Romans 5:5). Therefore, the Holy Spirit is a beautiful gift from God that you should welcome into your life.

*Dear Lord, thank You for the gift of the Holy Spirit that You sent in Your Son's name. I have been so blessed by His presence, and I am so grateful for His guidance. Please teach me to purely express His divine love. Amen.*

# 56

# Restore Them

Brothers and sisters, if someone is caught in a sin, you
who live by the Spirit should restore that person gently.
But watch yourselves, or you also may be tempted.

Galatians 6:1

We don't know the hearts, minds, or histories of others.
People often feel the way they feel, think the way they
think, and do what they do for reasons we cannot fully understand because we don't know the details of their past or present
situations. We are not even sure how we would respond under
similar circumstances. For instance, my childhood friend grew
up to be shamelessly promiscuous. People called her despicable
names. For years, I also wondered why she had multiple partners.
I grew up with her, and from what I could see, she had a decent
childhood. Well, one day when we were in our early twenties,
she confided in me. She told me she had been sexually abused by
a babysitter when she was three years old, and the abuse lasted
a couple of years. She told her story as if the abuse was a minor
bicycle accident.

As I sat there, feeling and looking uncomfortable, she said,
"I'm all right, though. It doesn't bother me."

After our conversation, we just went on about our day, doing what twenty-year-olds do, laughing at everything and nothing, like neither of us knew pain.

Today, twenty plus years later, I would handle that situation much differently. I would help her find a good therapist who specializes in the treatment of sexual abuse and suggest a number of helpful books she could read by Christian authors who are survivors of childhood sexual abuse. Sadly, I cannot help my friend now because her promiscuity led to her death. Unfortunately, while she was alive, no one realized she spent most of her life trying to forget the torment of her childhood. I certainly didn't realize it until it was too late. I never mentioned it again because I didn't want her to regret sharing her secret with me, so I went on with our friendship pretending the abuse didn't matter. Even if that was what she wanted, it was the wrong thing to do.

After I realized the magnitude of my mistake and the weight of my regret, I decided to help others by writing about it. I figured it was the best way for me to reach people without being intrusive. Some issues are uncomfortable and painful to discuss, like sexual abuse, but God still wants us to talk about it so the healing process can begin. If you or someone you know has been sexually abused, please get help. Go online and research agencies today. May God's grace help you through the restoration process.

*Dear Lord, please help victims of sexual abuse and rehabilitate perpetrators who have robbed others of their innocence. Lord, it is so hard for me to pray for the latter, but I know they are Your children too. Please teach me to be sensitive to everyone who needs restoration, and renew my strength in areas that have been weakened by life's circumstances. Amen.*

# 51

# God Healed My Body

But he was pierced for our transgressions, he was crushed
for our iniquities; the punishment that brought us peace
was on him, and by his wounds we are healed.

Isaiah 53:5

Tumors in my womb had gotten so large that my uterus was
the size of a sixth-month pregnancy. I had already had a UFE
(uterine fibroid embolization) seven years prior. The procedure
slowed the tumors down but did not stop them from growing.
My gynecologist told me I should seriously consider having a
hysterectomy. I figured he was probably right.

I had waited long enough, and the tumors were relentless.
Three weeks a month I felt horrible. I spent the first week so
bloated I felt like I was carrying around a soccer ball. The second week, I had severe cramps and a heavy menstrual flow. The
third week, I was weak and had a consistent headache from the
loss of blood. My symptoms convinced me that it was definitely
time to have surgery.

My doctor explained that my incision would have to start
above my navel. Since he had already given me bikini cuts with
my two c-sections, he had to do a vertical incision for the hyster-

ectomy. And, of course, the incision had to start above my navel
because the tumors were so large. I came to the realization that I
had three options: I could let the tumors continue to grow until
I reached menopause in eight to ten years, have the surgery, or
expect a healing.

The healing option was the most favorable of the three, but I
was running out of time because my symptoms were worsening
each month. I had heard of other people getting healed. I even
knew some of them, but I wasn't sure if God would do it for me.
I thought maybe I had to go through the process for reasons I did
not yet understand. I decided I would schedule my surgery for
summer if God did not miraculously heal me by spring.

In the meantime, I had a good friend—I mean a really good
*praying* friend—who told me not to believe the lies of the enemy.
I tried to look confident and secure in my beliefs as she spoke, but
it was a struggle. I was discouraged by my symptoms. My faith in
a healing "for me" was weakening, but while I was hanging on to
the little bit of faith I had concerning my healing, a familiar verse
came to mind: "'If you have faith as small as a mustard seed, you
can say to this mulberry tree, "Be uprooted and planted in the
sea," and it will obey you'" (Luke 17:6). Then I began to meditate
on Isaiah 53:5 and speak it throughout the day. I repeated, "By
his wounds, I am healed." My three miserable weeks continued
to come faithfully every month, but I took my mustard seed faith
and continued to combine it with God's Word.

While I was praying and waiting for my healing, I continued
to tutor, teach dance, and do poetry readings. My good friend
asked if I would speak at her church. It was a small church in the

Mt. Airy section of Philadelphia. As soon as I walked in the front door, I felt like I was a part of their family. We worshiped together and the atmosphere was filled with God's presence. When it was time for me to speak, I shared my testimony and read my work. They listened intently as I unfolded my life story. After I finished speaking, they asked if anyone in the room needed prayer. I raised my hand. The lady who laid hands on me explained that the tumors could not stay because the Holy Spirit lived inside me. She commanded them to shrink and repeated that they were "dead at the root." She had so much faith that I would be healed that it was contagious. More and more, I believed that I could be healed too. She even told me not to be amazed because this is just what God does.

Well, in the following months, I *was* amazed. The three horrible, debilitating weeks did not show up. I went to my doctor. He examined me and asked me to meet with him in his office. He compared his new notes with notes from my previous visit. His eyes widened. I don't know anything about his religious beliefs, but I could tell he was amazed too as he told me my fibroids shrank thirty percent and I no longer needed surgery. He explained that my tumors had been well above my navel and "now, they are below it." Well, I hit that man's desk with both hands, lowered my head, and said, "Thank you, Jesus. God is so . . . good."

I told my doctor about the service and how God had healed me. He nodded his head very calmly, maintaining his professionalism. Well, I left his office jumping on the inside. I was so excited and just so, so grateful. I got in my car and called my family and good friend. I had to get myself together before I drove home because I was so teary-eyed that I couldn't see well enough to drive. While driving, I kept thinking, *God healed me.*

It has been a few months since the doctor told me my tumors shrank thirty percent and I no longer needed surgery. When I press on my stomach now, I don't feel tumors above or below my navel. For the first time in my life, I am looking forward to my next yearly exam. My doctor is going to be even more amazed than he was the last time he saw me because God's work is truly amazing.

*Dear Lord, in Your Word You said, "'For where two or three gather in my name, there am I with them,'" (Matthew 18:20). Thank You for being there, Lord. Thank You for healing me. I also have readers who need to be healed. I want them to personally experience Your amazing healing powers. Please touch them where their minds and bodies hurt and restore their health. Amen.*

# 58

# Help Others

*. . . If anyone serves, they should do so with the strength God provides, so that in all things God may be praised through Jesus Christ. To him be the glory and the power for ever and ever. Amen.*

1 Peter 4:11

On the day of this writing, my son will be graduating from Rutgers-Camden's Honors College, magna cum laude, Phi Beta Kappa, with departmental honors. Both my husband and I cannot thank God enough for this moment in Jeffrey's life, but I must admit that the respect we have for our son has little to do with his academic accomplishments. We mostly respect him for making Jesus Christ the center of his life and starting a non-profit organization that helps the less fortunate members of our society. When people hear about his organization, they often ask how we raised such a caring young man. I tell them that my husband and I simply loved Christ, loved each other, and cared deeply for the people around us. Consequently, our actions made a much deeper impression on Jeffrey than we had imagined.

Jeffrey was a toddler when we first gave him a bag of fruit to hand to the homeless woman who knocked on the front door of our Camden home. He was in kindergarten when we first bagged up some of his toys and gave them to the neighborhood children. He was in grade school when we gave our Bible to a disheveled woman who was nodding on the corner. He was a pre-teen when we took the boys in our neighborhood to the mountains on a weekend vacation. He was a teenager when we gave our vehicle away to a needy family. He was twenty when he started Miracles Global, Inc., an organization that caters to the needs of underprivileged people.

Miracles has had successful clothing and school supply drives, partnered with Rutgers to raise money for Haiti, volunteered on Cooper Hospital's Children's Unit, and offered free tutoring services for students in the inner city. For this, we are most proud of our son. However, with our pride comes a huge amount of humility. My husband and I both know that we could not have raised Jeffrey successfully on our own. Jesus gets full credit. So as I write on this morning, the dawn of my son's graduation, I would like to give God glory for Jeffrey's accomplishments, and I would especially like to thank God for giving him a heart of compassion.

When you pray for children, remember: they are much more than grades, awards, and personal achievements. There is nothing wrong with praying for children's success, but it is also important to ask God to make them kindhearted people who consistently help others. The same goes for you. Your titles and degrees are of little value if you are only using them for personal gain. Use what you have to be a blessing to other people.

> *Dear God, remind me that I have the strength, ability, and resources to help others because Your restoration power resides in me. For every amount of success You have given me, please give me a double portion of humility so I am never reluctant to help others. Amen.*

# 59

# Compassion for All

The Lord is good to all; he has compassion on all he
has made.

Psalm 145:9

"I sat anxiously in the examination room as the doctor studied
my x-rays. His pen traced the area of concern. . . . He insisted
on surgery as soon as possible. I was too surprised to protest, and
I left the hospital with an operation scheduled for the summer
before eighth grade."

The excerpt above is from my daughter's essay. I cannot fully
express how difficult it was for *me* during that time of her life.
I talked to God multiple times within the hour, every hour. I
prayed ceaselessly that she would be able to walk again. I got down
on my knees every day by my bedside and prayed. Sometimes
I would just repeat, "Lord, I trust you." Then one day, through
my tears, I saw visions of her walking at what appeared to be her
eighth grade, high school, and college graduations.

Hallelujah! My visions became reality. God restored her
strength and her ability to walk, and even though she missed a
third of the school year, she graduated from middle school with
the highest average in her eighth grade class. Next she went on

to high school, and April of her senior year she received her acceptance letter from Princeton University. Then in June, she graduated as the class valedictorian. I was full of gratitude as Jade walked confidently up to the podium to deliver her farewell speech, smiling broader than I had ever seen her smile.

She spoke candidly to the class of graduating seniors: "The more educated and the more successful we become, the greater our responsibility to maintain our humility and help combat the poverty, illness, disparity, and lack of education we witnessed firsthand during our hours of required service. We must remember . . . the victims of natural disasters, poverty, and disease. . . . We must remember the lessons we have learned about emulating Christ and easing the suffering of others through service. If we can remember this, not only will we appreciate the gift we have been given today, but also become invariably more sensitive to the needs of others."

When Jade says "others," she is referring to both people and non-human animals. She is intensely aware of the injustices and suffering of God's creatures, especially those who are unable to speak for themselves. Thus, she is a vegan and spends several hours a week volunteering for the Humane Society. Although she is also a human activist, she believes her essential purpose in life is to fight against animal cruelty. The same determination that helped her through the most difficult physical and societal circumstances will help her in her mission to improve the lives of some of God's most vulnerable creatures.

*Dear God, please remind me that any living thing that You have given a nervous system feels pain. I do not want to cause or support the suffering of any being. Please give me compassion for all You have made. Amen.*

# 60

# New Generations

... "Who am I, Lord God, and what is my family, that you
have brought me this far?"

1 Chronicles 17:16

Since I have fully committed my life to Christ, I have often
asked God a similar question. I understand how David felt,
both grateful and undeserving. God has been so wonderful to me
and my family since we surrendered our lives to him. It's sometimes unbelievable because my husband and I come from, as it
is romantically called, humble beginnings. However, if I had to
give our start a more candid term, it would simply be called the
ghetto. Even beyond that, our parents and grandparents were
either poor, dysfunctional, or both. We both came from child-
hoods that were plagued by addiction and abuse. Statistically, we
should not be where we are today, but, divinely, we are exactly
where God wants us to be.

My husband, my children, and I have had our struggles, but
even through the most difficult times of our Christian lives, we
have felt God's presence. Through depression, sickness, and death,
God has been our healer, our reliever of intolerable hurts. Besides
sustaining us through our trials, God has also been there to cel-

ebrate our victories. He is our divine parent Who cheers us on. So, who are we that God is so concerned about us? We are His children, who decided to trust Him with our lives.

*Dear Lord, my family and I cannot thank You enough for breaking a familial history of poverty and abuse. Thank You for restoring us and breaking every curse that plagued our past relatives. Now, Lord, I am asking You to please do that for the reader of this devotional. Touch them and help them break away from a past of brokenness so their family can be blessed beyond human ability. Lead them through life's joys and struggles and anoint their new beginning with You. Amen.*

For more information about
SHAWN R. JONES
&
PICTURES IN GLASS FRAMES
please visit:

*www.shawnrjones.com*
*facebook.com/shawn.r.jones*
*sjjjones@msn.com*

For more information about
AMBASSADOR INTERNATIONAL
please visit:

*www.ambassador-international.com*
*@AmbassadorIntl*
*www.facebook.com/AmbassadorIntl*